Succeeding with LD*

with LD*

SPECIAL SECTION Ten Years Later

TRUE STORIES
ABOUT REAL PEOPLE WITH LD*

*Learning Differences

Jill Lauren, M.A.

With a Message to Parents and Teachers from
Dr. Harold S. Koplewicz

Star Bright Books
New York

This book is dedicated to three incredible people:
Dr. Doris Johnson and Dee Klein, two warm and wise professors at
Northwestern University who have greatly influenced my teaching;
and Margaret Babyak, a smart and courageous student who helped
me realize that this book needed to be written.

Text copyright © 2008, 2003, 1997 Jill Lauren, with exceptions noted below. All rights reserved. Unless otherwise noted (see pages 118-119), no part of this book may be reproduced or transmitted in any form or by any means, electronic or mechanical, photocopying, recording, or by any information storage and retrieval systems that are available now or in the future, without permission in writing from the copyright holder and the publisher.

Published in the United States of America by Star Bright Books, Inc., New York. The name Star Bright Books and the Star Bright Books logo are registered trademarks. Please visit www.starbrightbooks.com.

ISBN-13: 978-1-59572-106-8
Printed in India (NU) 9 8 7 6 5 4 3 2 1

Library of Congress Cataloging-in-Publication Data

Lauren, Jill, 1961-
  Succeeding with LD : true stories about real people with LD / Jill Lauren ; with a
message to parents and teachers by Dr. Harold Koplewicz.
    p. cm.
  ISBN 978-1-59572-106-8 (pbk.)
  1. Learning disabled--United States--Biography. 2. Learning disabled children--United States--
Biography. 3. Learning disabled--Education--United States. 4. Learning disabled children--
Education--United States--Biography. I. Title.
  LC4818.5.L38 2008
  371.9092'2--dc22
  [B]
                                        2008003512

The photos of John (Jack) Horner on the cover and pages 20 and 24 are used by permission of the Museum of the Rockies. The photo of John (Jack) Horner with Steven Spielberg on page 22 is used by permission of Amblin Entertainment. The photo of John (Jack) Horner on the Jurassic Park set on page 23 is used by permission of Universal Pictures. The story about Samuel R. Delany that appears on pages 53-58 by Samuel R. Delany and Jill Lauren (copyright © 1996 by Samuel R. Delany and Jill Lauren) appears here by permission of the authors and Samuel R. Delany's agent, Henry Morrison, Inc. Page 58: Photo by Phillipe Dollo. Page 70: Photo © Cal Poly, San Luis Obispo. Text excerpted from COPY THIS! © 2005 by The Orfalea Family Foundation. Used by permission of Workman Publishing Co., Inc. New York. All rights reserved. The images by Pat Buckley Moss, *Winter Serenade* on page 85, and *To Our Heroes* on page 86 (copyright © 1993 and 2006 P. Buckley Moss, respectively) are used courtesy of the artist and the Moss Portfolio. No reproduction, lamination, mounting, trimming, matting, or framing may be made using the Moss image contained herein. The image may not be used, in whole or in part, for any other product. To do so violates P. Buckley Moss's copyright, trademark, and trade dress rights. The publisher would like to thank Pat Buckley Moss and the Moss Portfolio for permission to reprint the photos of the artist on pages 80, 81, 83, and of her signature on page 84. Cover, page 102: Photo by Nate DeMarse, FDNY Squad 61.

Acknowledgments

Without a doubt, this book could not have been written without the help of many people. I have to thank the twenty-one individuals profiled in the book for sharing their stories. While these people are being celebrated for their successes, the success usually came after great hardship and pain. It was not uncommon for someone to cry during an interview or wince at an uncomfortable memory. Each person honestly and openly shared his or her life with me so that other individuals with LD might be inspired or relieved by of success. Thank you Eileen, Justin, David S., Anitra, Daiana, David C., Robert, Lucia, Megan, Carlos, Gavin, John Jr., April, John III, Pat, Garth, Liz, Jack, Peggy, Sam, and Paul. Your stories are indeed a gift.

I have many people to thank for helping me to find the students and adults profiled. These teachers and colleagues recognized the importance of such a book for the LD community and freely gave me their time and energy. Their efforts will certainly benefit many. Thank you Susan King, Alice Pulliam, Lorraine Fitz, Nancy White, Ann Roldan, Jim O'Toole, Kim Lonas, Kelly Perry-Sanchez, Jackie Long, Richard Soghoian, Robert Shaw, Lynn Flinders, Lisa Grunow, William Adams, Helen Steinberg, Kathy Schwartz, Tricia Miles, Cindy Scruggs, Marilyn Stein, Nancy Carlinsky, Jo Ellen Gordon, Beverly Metcalf, Malcolm Henderson, Laura McCormack, Iris Spano, and Marcy Dann-Rathbone. Dr. Larry Silver and Dr. Regina Cicci provided important feedback on the "Ten Questions and Answers About LD" section of this book. Dr. Sheldon Horowitz, Anne Ford, and Dr. G. Reid Lyon furnished valuable review and comments. Dr. Judith Rosenberger edited the forward for the third addition. Again, thank you.

Dr. Harold Koplewicz's "A Message to Parents and Teachers" beautifully highlights aspects of resiliency that are critical for success among individuals with learning differences. He writes with grace and provides helpful information about children with disabilities. Quite simply, I am thrilled that his words are part of my book. Thank you, Dr. Koplewicz, for your support of this project.

I remain indebted to Judy Galbraith of Free Spirit Publishing for creating the first two editions of *Succeeding with LD*, and to Ellen Reeves of the New Press for bringing the book to Judy's attention. The third edition arrives because of the commitment of Deborah Shine of Star Bright Books to people with disabilities. Deborah and her staff, especially Tina Trent, have carefully put together a beautiful new book that will not only benefit folks with LD, but is also an important addition to the field of LD as it serves as a qualitative long term study. Thank you to Star Bright for believing in this book.

Finally, wonderful Charlie, who is a much better writer than I, edited all the profiles for the third edition.

Jill Lauren
New York City, 2008

CONTENTS

Anitra Simpson 8

Anitra has trouble understanding and using language. She was in special education classes for years but worked hard to move into a few regular education classes. Now Anitra works for a home improvement company.

Justin Quan 13

Justin had a hard time learning to read and write, but after working very hard was able to read above grade level. Justin is now in college.

Dr. John R. Horner 17

Dr. John (Jack) Horner had trouble with every subject in school and flunked out of college. Today, he is a brilliant paleontologist at the top of his field. He received a MacArthur Foundation Award (also known as the "Genius Award") and was the real-life model for the paleontologist in the movie Jurassic Park. *He lives and teaches in Montana.*

Peggy Jorgensen 25

Peggy has trouble with numbers but loves to read and write. As a teacher, she wants to make all her students feel good about themselves because she recalls what it was like when her teachers yelled at her for her math weakness. Peggy lives in Connecticut and is also a real estate agent.

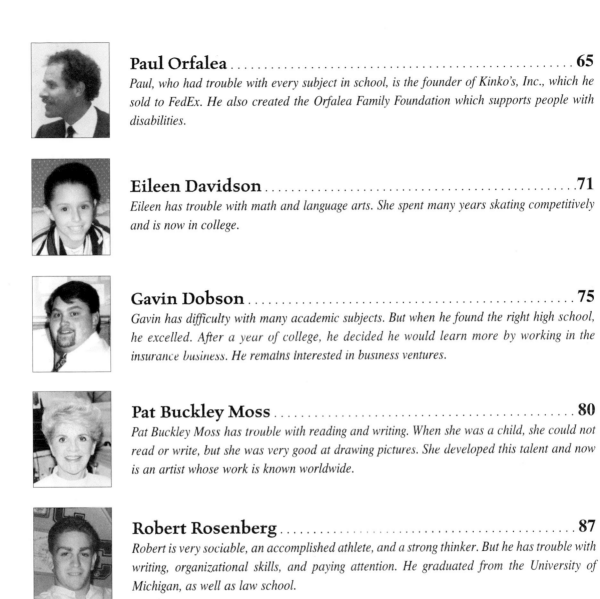

David Collado **96**

David has a hard time with reading, writing, and organizational skills. He is very talented in video production, computer graphics, and music. David works as a firefighter in New York City.

Dr. Garth Vaz **103**

Garth has difficulty with reading and writing, but is strong in math, science, and understanding people. In medical school, he was asked to leave because he told a professor he had dyslexia, and the school thought he would be incapable of becoming a doctor. Garth refused to accept that and instead worked hard to show his knowledge. Today, he practices medicine in Texas.

Elizabeth Davis **109**

Elizabeth (who goes by Liz) has been diagnosed as dyslexic. She is a strong listener, speaker, and thinker. Despite being told that she would never graduate from high school, she made it all the way through law school. Liz runs her own company, which specializes in emergency management.

Introduction

You are about to meet some amazing people. All of them have something in common: School was difficult for them. Each day, they went to school and felt the frustration of not understanding what their teachers were teaching. This frustration often left them feeling that they were "stupid," though deep down inside they knew they were not. The reason they experienced difficulty in school was because of something else they have in common—LD.

There are different names for LD, some of which you have probably heard. LD can mean "learning difference," "learning disability," "learning disorder," or "learning difficulty." Students, parents, and teachers often simply call it LD.

A learning disability can be confusing to understand—how can someone be smart and at the same time have trouble learning? It is because people with learning differences have strengths in certain subjects but weaknesses in others. So, some subjects will naturally be easier, and some will be more difficult.

Why do some people have LD? Because the minds of people with LD work in a unique way. Scientists are discovering more each day about how our minds work, and know that the LD mind works differently. Each person with LD receives, understands, and/or expresses certain kinds of information in a way that is different from other people. At the end of this book, you'll find some basic information on LD. There is also a list of recommended books, videos, organizations, and websites that can help you better understand LD. These resources may answer your questions, and offer the advice or information you're looking for.

LD affects each person uniquely. For example, some of the people you'll meet in this book have difficulty reading and writing but are very strong in math. Some have a hard time memorizing facts but are great at expressing ideas. Paying attention is very difficult for some, while others can't learn a foreign language. Some find it hard to listen to their teachers lecture or to sit still. Going to school each day and dealing with these challenges can be very demanding.

Even though learning has been tough for the people profiled in this book, they all realized that they had strengths in certain areas. They chose to focus on their strengths instead of on their weaknesses, and that made them feel good about themselves. You will see how this choice, combined with a determination to work hard, led to their success. In fact, a few of the people profiled in the book believe that their LD makes them special.

Everyone in the book is successful although they had, or still have, a great deal of difficulty with certain subjects or skills. They all have something else in common—their LD meant that they had to work unbelievably hard. They didn't let their LD keep them from following a dream or reaching a goal. Believing you can succeed, even when life is challenging, takes a great deal of courage and persistence.

If you have LD, think about your learning difficulties as you read these stories. You are probably very aware of what is hard for you. But be sure to also think about what you do well. Many individuals in this book believe that focusing on a strength helped them get through tougher times. Are you spending enough time working on and enjoying your own strengths?

If you don't have LD, these stories can help you better understand what it's like to have LD. Do you have a friend or family member with LD? Think of the people in your school, classroom, and neighborhood. Is there someone you know who has a great deal of trouble learning, or who seems a lot like one of the people in this book? Maybe someone you know goes to the resource room at school, or is in an LD program, but you never knew why. This book will show you that LD affects people of all ages, genders, races, and backgrounds. More importantly, this book can help you realize that although people with LD have difficulty in school, they each have a unique strength and can go as far as they want in life.

Whether you have LD or not, the stories in this book can inspire you to try new things and to reach your goals. What steps can you take to follow your dream? Is there someone in your life who can help you get better at something you've dreamed of doing? This person can be a parent, a relative, or a teacher. Your friends can also help you with your goals. Many of the people you'll read about here have very supportive friends.

Reading this book may also help you think of a way to reach a goal you haven't yet considered. Maybe one of the kids or adults in the stories has accomplished something you'd like to do. Go ahead and give it a try. Find a way to explore something you're interested in; discover your talent and work hard to show it off.

The message in the individual stories is clear: Focus on your abilities while you continue to work hard on the areas that give you trouble. Even though learning a certain subject or skill may be difficult for you, keep trying and don't give up. Find people who can support you as you learn and grow. Each story in this book is special and inspirational. And everyone in this book hopes that their story will help you think about what you can achieve.

Jill Lauren
New York City, 1997

Ten Years Later…

Ten years ago, a remarkable group of people with LD agreed to publicly share their hardships and triumphs, hoping that telling their stories would help others. They did help. Across the country, people read about ten-year-old Eileen and remembered how hard, if not impossible, it had been for them to learn multiplication facts. They read about Jack's passion for dinosaurs, which inspired them to explore hobbies that they enjoyed. Children and adults with dyslexia related to Pat's embarrassing moments and identified with her retreat into art as a way to escape her shame. Each person's struggles and achievements resonated with, and inspired, many other individuals with LD.

Since the publication of the first edition of this book, many readers asked what happened to the people profiled. It became clear to me that by speaking with the people I interviewed ten years ago and updating their stories, I could present readers with a deeper understanding of how, and why, LD need not preclude success in life, including the attainment of career goals. In this third edition, the original stories are followed by updated profiles reflecting events of the last ten years.

Research on learning disabilities often reveals the disheartening impact of LD throughout many aspects of life. It is extraordinary, then, that there was an almost unanimous willingness to once again share personal experiences for a third edition in order to inspire others. The profiles illustrate many aspects of resiliency that are important to note. For example, the individuals in this book remain honest about how LD still affects their lives and how they work around it. Also, many of them discuss finding careers that capitalize on their strengths, thereby indicating how continued self-awareness is critical to their happiness.

I am also gratified by the fact that many of the persons revisited in this third edition of *Succeeding with LD* express a level of confidence that might be unexpected from people often judged to be "stupid" simply because they learn differently than others. Their past achievements continue to propel them—a powerful reminder that we must find ways to help all people with LD experience a sense of success and pride, both in and out of school.

These profiles also highlight other significant aspects of life with LD. Almost everyone, once again, mentions teachers or programs that made a difference. Their stories show how teachers who care clearly create an indelible impression that will be remembered and felt for a lifetime. On the other hand, there is a real sense of anger—still fresh—towards individual teachers, coaches, or others who were unduly judgmental or critical. Perhaps most significant over the last ten years has been the influence of technology in helping to circumvent some of the obstacles faced by persons with LD. While computers are critical in their ability to help level the playing field, the prospects of success can only increase when the individual understands his or her specific learning profile, gets the needed help, and continues to work tenaciously.

Succeeding with LD is not a story of miracles. Rather, it reveals how hard work, insight, appropriate technology, and other tools can transform hopelessness into hope, and points to the specific kinds of learning and teaching that make success possible. Congratulations to Anitra, Justin, Jack, Peggy, Carlos, John Jr., April, John III, David S., Megan, Sam, Daiana, Paul, Eileen, Gavin, Pat, Robert, Lucia, David C., Garth, and Elizabeth for pursuing dreams and finding satisfaction. Once again, we thank them for sharing their stories about LD so that others might learn and be inspired.

Jill Lauren
New York City, 2008

A Message to Parents and Teachers

As parents are deluged with information about the problems of children with learning difficulties, they may get so involved in defining their child's "disability" that they lose sight of their child's positive attributes. We're all too familiar with stories about young persons who become discouraged and think they're stupid, lazy, or crazy. But let's not lose sight of those who are able to carve out productive and satisfying lives, despite their difficulties.

In the first edition of *Succeeding with LD*, an extraordinary book, Jill Lauren profiled individuals of all ages with learning problems whose belief in themselves gave them the courage to mobilize their strengths and to work hard to compensate for difficulties. Ten years later, Ms. Lauren revisited the individuals she originally interviewed to discuss their experiences in the intervening years. She chronicled the obstacles, frustrations and accomplishments of their individual journeys, thus helping us to appreciate their lives and accomplishments with a deeper, more nuanced understanding.

What do these stories tell us about the qualities and experiences that enable some people to overcome obstacles and to capitalize on strengths while others struggle? Each story is uniquely compelling, but the threads that run through them are striking. One thread is the unwavering support of parents, teachers, and other adults. With a secure, supportive base, students are empowered to meet life's challenges with an optimistic "I can do it" attitude. Another related thread is seen in each individual's capacity for resilience; they all exhibit the ability to bounce back after adversity. Each story also depicts people who were able to identify their problems, while they also recognized and utilized their strengths. When faced with obstacles, these qualities helped them sustain their motivation and their self-esteem.

Ms. Lauren's ten-year follow-up interviews help us understand human resilience and the diversity of human experience. The range of individual goals and definitions of success are made real in stories as varied as Anitra's success as a receptionist, Robert's completion of both college and law school, Jack's career as a paleontologist, and April's accomplishments in real estate. In addition to giving us insight into the minds and hearts of these unusual people, these narratives remind us that life in the classroom can be stressful and degrading for those who learn in nontraditional ways.

This new edition of *Succeeding with LD*, with its ten-year perspective, provides some unexpected benefits. By introducing us to people of all ages with learning problems, Ms.

Lauren has done the world of education a service. These stories of courage and determination serve as models to promote respect for diverse learning styles. Most importantly, the stories help us recognize that differences exist among people, differences that make each person's narrative special. The people profiled also refused to be defined by their learning problems, and their response to their challenges provides insight into helpful strategies.

Unfortunately, individual success stories are not as common as they should be. Current educational research has shown the shortcomings of the traditional 'one-size-fits-all' teaching approach. Learning differences are generally not appreciated, and for many students the classroom remains a humiliating environment. Current statistics call attention to the need for changes in our educational system. The number of children diagnosed as learning disabled has tripled in recent years. According to a study by the National Assessment of Adult Literacy (2005) by the U.S. Department of Education, thirty million people are unable to read basic text, such as directions or medical instructions, due to undiagnosed learning disabilities, inadequate schooling, and parents who were themselves poor readers.

As a child and adolescent psychiatrist, I often see children and families who are dealing with the realization that their child may need help in mastering academic work. My priorities, in addition to making sure that the family works with the school to develop an appropriate educational plan, are to help the family create a climate that will build on the child's special strengths to enable him/her to develop a strong, flexible sense of self and an optimistic point of view. Another important aspect of my work with my colleagues at the New York University Child Study Center is to further research and to utilize recent advances in technology, such as brain scans and functional MRIs, that provide new scientific insights as to how learning occurs – how information enters the brain, is processed, stored, and then used. It is with this advanced scientific knowledge that new perceptions and educational procedures will be developed. The future definitely looks bright.

We are truly indebted to Ms. Lauren and the courageous people she profiles in *Succeeding with LD* who were willing to share their personal journeys in the hope that their experiences will light the path for others who are struggling.

Harold S. Koplewicz, M.D.
Founder and Director of the NYU Child Study Center;
Arnold and Debbie Simon Professor and Chair,
Department of Child and Adolescent Psychiatry;
NYU Langone Medical Center

Success Stories

Anitra Simpson

Age 15

Anitra Simpson's ninth grade class picture.

▶

Anitra, who lives in Maryland, has trouble understanding and using language. She was in special education classes for years but has worked hard to move into a few regular education classes. Anitra loves art and uses her artistic talents when she studies.

School was hard for me from the very first day of first grade. I didn't want to be there, so I kicked and bit the teacher. My mother took me home, but I was back the next day.

I had difficulty with language—it was hard to find the words. Remembering and pronouncing the words in reading was hard. I was tested constantly, and I remember wondering, "Why are they doing this? What did I do wrong?" I repeated first grade and was then placed in small special education classes for the rest of elementary school.

Anitra with her mother and father.
◀

My teachers began to help me understand that words are hard for me and that I had a little problem. The English language is difficult. It was tough to get things correct because there are so many different ways of saying things, like past tense and present tense. The teachers helped me to understand this. There was always a nice teacher telling me everything straight up.

My special ed classes were the best thing that ever happened to me. You get more attention, and the teacher is always around. When I was reading, I would get to the end and say, "What just happened? How can I absorb what's happening and read at the same time?" My teachers taught me strategies to help me understand what I read. Every line or two lines, I would stop and review.

I would also draw pictures about the story. I love art, so that really helped. Writing was hard, but I loved to write stories. I learned how to organize my

Do you have difficulty with language, like Anitra does? What strategies might help you?

Are you an artist, like Anitra? What types of art do you most enjoy? Who is your favorite artist?

Best School Memory

"My first day taking a regular ed class."

Worst School Memory

"Breaking my tooth in second grade."

ideas, and sometimes I would make a story outline. My handwriting was good, and I even got an award for my cursive writing.

Ever since the first grade, I've been interested in art. My mom would buy me crayons and paper, and I would just draw and color. When I got older and was tired of pens, pencils, and studying, I'd just get out a crayon and color. I'd use all the colors and try them all out. Colors make me feel good, especially blue. Blue is bold, very curious—it's just really classic. Color is really about me. I'm bright, and all the colors are just really me, all in one.

In fifth grade, I displayed my artwork for the first time. One of my pieces won an award, and I couldn't believe it. After this, I decided to look outside of my own work and see how other artists work. My art has gotten better, and I can do more with a pencil. When I started drawing, I did it for me. No one could really judge it or test me on it, and I liked that.

By the end of fifth grade, after working really hard in special ed, I began to wonder what it would be like in regular ed. I felt I could do the work. When I entered middle school, I was again placed in all special ed classes. My special ed classes continued to help me be as smart as I could be. I finally got the rhythm of what was going on, and I got on the honor roll for the first time. My teachers decided it was time for me to try a regular ed class. I really wanted to do this, but I was also scared.

My first regular ed class was world studies. It was hard to keep up, but I was patient and I listened very carefully. At first, my grades were low compared to the rest of the class.

The teacher helped me understand the material, and I would stay after class if I had questions. I would meet with him before school, after school, or at lunch if needed. Then my grades began to improve, and he told me that I was exactly where I needed to be. I felt great.

For the rest of middle school, I had mostly special ed classes and one or two regular ed classes. My regular ed classes, such as eighth grade science, were the hardest. There was so much work, and it was so "heavy." But all I had to do was ask, and the teacher would be willing to spend extra time with me.

I would never ask for extra help in front of my friends. I didn't want my regular ed friends to know about my special ed classes. They probably would have looked at me weird and said, "I can't believe Anitra has special ed classes."

Anitra holds up two of her paintings.

I think the kids in regular ed think the special ed kids aren't smart. Many regular ed kids think that everyone has to be on one level and if you're not, there's something wrong. I'm more comfortable with my special ed friends because I don't really have to think about what I want to say or if I said it right. With my regular ed friends, I'm still a little embarrassed.

By the time I went to high school, my teachers and I had decided that I was ready for more regular ed classes. I told them, "Put the work in front of me, and I'll do it." Now, in ninth grade, I have only two special ed classes. The work is hard, and I'm working all the time. You have to stay on top of things and ask the teacher for help when you need it. I'm constantly reviewing and studying, reviewing and studying. I still draw pictures to help me when I study, and I really hate tests.

My report card is mostly A's and B's. Maybe I'll get to where I'll have all regular ed classes, but not anytime soon. I'm very comfortable where I am. I'm also grateful for all the help from my special ed teachers. I have no idea what I want to do in college, but I know I don't want to do art as a career. It's something special to do on the side.

?? ?

Anitra feels that her friends in regular education classes might look down on her for being in special ed. Have you been in a situation like this? What could you say to someone who thinks kids in special ed are not smart?

"I want to say to all kids everywhere, stay in school. Do all of your work on time and respect your classmates and teachers. Don't pay attention to what people say you can't do—go out and prove yourself! Don't let anyone put you down. Say what you feel and don't be afraid. Be yourself, love yourself, and be strong!"

Anitra

WHERE'S ANITRA NOW?

By the end of ninth grade, I was out of special ed classes. It was scary taking all regular ed classes, but I learned not to be afraid to ask questions. I wanted to grasp and understand the information—I just had to have that knowledge. If something was hard, I always, always stayed after class or met with the teacher on her lunch break. It was like a private one-on-one session.

In college, things became easier for me. I learned how to search through many resources for information. I opened lots of books, got on the Internet and kept asking questions. I knew how to really apply myself and study hard. I even made Dean's List.

Language is easier for me, but sometimes I get stuck finding the word I want and ask, "What do you call that?" You'd be surprised how people help you to figure out what you're trying to say. I listen to language around me when I'm out and about and try to pick up new words. Reading helps me to pick up new vocabulary, too. I do love English, and sometimes I've thought about being an English teacher.

I do less art now, but I still make creative birthday presents such as scrapbooks. I also write poetry, go to church, and listen to the soulful sounds of gospel music. I really enjoy reading inspiring books and quotes from influential women and men. Two years ago, I finally had the financial earnings to treat myself to my dream car, a 1999 Ford Mustang.

At work, I've been promoted from my job as a receptionist. Now I'm in accounts receivable, which is not easy. I'm still getting trained, and I do make mistakes. Since I'm really good at taking notes, I refer to them if I'm stuck. This has been so helpful. There are other departments where I might put my toe one day and see what I can get out of that. I don't ever second guess myself or let my past hold me back from my future. For me, the key to happiness is to get out, play, and try lots of new things. The sky's the limit.

Justin Quan
Age 12

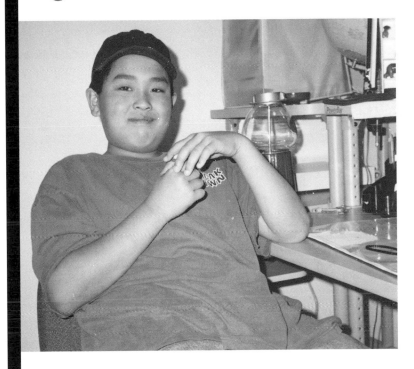

Justin Quan at home in his bedroom.

◀

Justin had a hard time learning to read and write, but after working very hard, he is now reading above his grade level. In his spare time, Justin likes to build sports equipment. He lives in California.

Do you remember when you first learned to read? How are your reading skills now? What do you do to become a better reader?

Does your LD make you mad? Justin took a walk when he got mad. What physical activity helps you feel better when you're angry, upset, or sad?

Second grade was the worst. I remember all the other kids were reading. My teacher told me to just go and sit in the corner because I couldn't read. The teachers made such a big deal about reading. Reading was everything, and I didn't know how to do it.

Once, my teacher gave me a book and told me to try and read it. That didn't work. I would be sitting in the corner watching the other kids and thinking, "Why can't I be like them?" My teacher said I'd eventually learn how to read, but she didn't show me how. I felt frustrated and miserable.

Second grade was so bad that I didn't want to be there. When I woke up in the morning, I would tell my mom that I didn't want to go to school. It wasn't fun, and I went through a lot of pressure. For a while, I was worried that I might not ever learn how to read, and then I thought I would be stupid.

I thought the other kids must be smarter than me. Sometimes I would come home crying. My parents would comfort me. They told me that I'd be OK. Sometimes, if I'd had a bad day, I'd be really irritable. I'd get mad real fast, and I didn't want to talk about what was bothering me. Then I just told my parents how I felt. I needed time to work it out.

During second grade, I would sometimes come home and build stuff. I always liked to build things. When I was building things, I felt like I could do it. I built a fort with my dad, which helped me see that I could do something.

In the summer between second and third grade, my parents took me to a doctor who told me I had dyslexia. I was in denial. I didn't want to have any problems. I felt terrible. Then they told me that I was going to the public school near my house because there was a special teacher who knew how to teach me to read.

In third grade, during reading time, I went to the resource room. In the beginning, I didn't like it. There were no other kids that I knew there. I was in the resource room for up to three hours a day, and sometimes I just didn't want to be there. I wouldn't work. I'd just mess around and disturb the class. I did it so I would get more attention, and then the teacher would help me more. If I got angry, she'd tell me to take a walk. That helped.

Finally, I decided I would try because I wanted to learn how to read. I knew I'd eventually learn. I saw a kid who couldn't read suddenly start reading. So I knew it could be done. My parents said I could do it, too. My resource room teacher, Mrs. Pulliam, showed me how to read. She helped me sound the words out. I remember the day I learned how to read. I said to my teacher, "I can do it!" I was so excited, I ran home and told my mom. I said, "I can read!" She said, "Good for you!"

Once I knew how to do it, reading became easier. I also learned how to write in third grade. It was hard at first because the letters were confusing. But then I got the hang of it. It was fun to work with Mrs. Pulliam because she could teach me. She told me that I could do it, and I believed her.

When my reading and writing improved, I spent less time in the resource room. I felt good about it because that told me in my head that I could do it, and I was very happy. In fourth grade, in the resource room, I learned more about writing. My teacher showed me how to brainstorm. She said I should think about things a little bit at a time. She also showed me a trick to remember the steps of long division. Each year, I spent less time in the resource room. Now I'm in sixth grade, and I only spend 45 minutes a day in the resource room. Mostly, I do my homework there. I also get help with grammar, but I hate grammar because it can be so confusing for me.

In sixth grade, I'm getting B's, and I'm going to do a better job on my grammar so I can get better grades. I feel good about what I can do. I have been reading above grade level for some time now. I had to work hard to get to this point, but it was worth it. You have to want to do it and believe in yourself. I knew I could do it because I had done other things before, such as building stuff.

I still build things. I just built a bike, and I'm going to build a half-pipe ramp for rollerblading. I know I'm going to college someday. Maybe I'll be an emergency room doctor, like on *ER*. But it's too hard to decide now. Now I just want to get good at snowboarding.

One of Justin's favorite sports is snowboarding.

Best School Memory
"The first day I learned how to read, when I ran home and told my mom."

Worst School Memory
"When I had to go sit in the corner while everyone else was reading."

Think of a teacher who has helped you learn something that was very hard for you. Is there a way to show your appreciation?

"Never give up. Just keep on trying."

justin

WHERE'S JUSTIN NOW?

High school started out pretty rough. First I went to a public school because I didn't get into a private school. I was often ridiculed for my LD and sometimes even beaten up. The school talked about putting me into a physically and mentally handicapped class, not because of my LD, but because of my mindset about school. I'd do my work, and then I'd go to the lunchroom and sit in the corner. I just didn't fit in because I was letting my LD float around me like a stigma that wouldn't go away. I felt like the kid who gets stuck in the resource room and isn't allowed to play at recess. I was just deteriorating and withering away.

So, the next two years I went to a boarding school. The classes were small, and I knew everyone. They had counseling and social groups. But I still didn't feel like I fit in. There was a lot of drinking and drugs. I was really freaked out. Most nights I would just study alone. School was still so hard, and in a lot of ways I had to grow up a lot earlier because of the drug situation. The school just wasn't prepared to handle kids with very, very specific issues, though they had told us they could.

Then I transferred to a school for kids with LD in Illinois called Brehm. It was the best experience because it was so much better to be around kids like myself. The teachers at Brehm taught me strategies to compensate for my weaknesses. When it was hard for me to keep up with note taking, I started using Inspiration software, which helped me with outlining. I used lots of books on tape and on iTunes, and a speech recognition program called Via-Voice. My academic performance improved because the classes were geared towards my learning disability. Learning specialists like Suzie Ventura and Char Reed gave me more insight into how my LD affected me socially and in school. I think students have to understand and accept their LD before they can really improve.

One thing I noticed at Brehm was that there was a lack of student government, so the students' voices could not be heard. With the assistance of the speech and language pathologist, I resurrected a student government. My senior year was probably my best because I became president of the school. I also took a college business class, with Brehm's support services to guide me, and did well. I was chosen to give the graduation speech.

I received a college scholarship, but after one year out East I came back to Brehm's college program. I get the accommodations I need, such as only having to take one test or quiz a day so my memory is not overloaded. I'm thinking about majoring in marketing or recreation and leisure management. I'm transferring to a four-year college now, but it can be hard for kids with LD to make that commitment. I know it will help with my employability and career goals, but school has already been hard enough. I will not stop going, though, until I'm ready.

Dr. John R. Horner
Age 49

Dr. John R. Horner
holds the upper jaw of a
Tyrannosaurus rex.

Dr. John (Jack) Horner had trouble with every subject in school and flunked out of college. Today, he is a brilliant paleontologist at the top of his field. He has received a MacArthur Foundation Award (some people call it the "Genius Award") and was the real-life model for the paleontologist in the movie Jurassic Park. He lives and teaches in Montana but looks for dinosaur bones all over the world.

Jack at age 8, when he found his first dinosaur bone.

Do you have a special interest you think about all the time? What do you do to explore it? How can you get more information about this interest?

I remember as far back as second grade having difficulty in school. I was terrible at math, terrible at reading, and terrible with foreign languages—which I thought included English. I was terrible at everything. People didn't understand LD when I went to school. My teachers thought I was lazy. But I knew I wasn't. I thought they meant I just wasn't very smart.

I was very interested in science. When I was eight years old, my father took me to a place near my home in Montana where he remembered a bunch of bones sticking out of the ground. While I was there, I picked up a bone and gave it a number because I was already cataloguing fossils. I thought it was a dinosaur bone and found out later that it was. I was so interested in dinosaurs and science that I thought about that stuff all the time, even in school.

In seventh and eighth grade, I remember wanting school to be over so I could get to the library. I looked at every science book in the town I lived in. Not only the ones in the library but also in the school, and in the libraries of the teachers and doctors. Every book I could find, everywhere. I never read them, because I couldn't read. The pictures helped me learn a lot about science, though.

I also spent a lot of time wandering around the hills of Montana, looking for bones and fossils. If I could get some friends to go with me, that was good. But I didn't need to—I entertained myself pretty easily. I was still having a terrible time learning in school. But my mind was filled with questions about science, so I wasn't worrying about failing classes.

High school was the place where I could put my questions about science into action. Every year, we had science fairs. During my freshman year, I made a big rocket that went a long way. Everyone knew about my rocket, and I won the science fair. I didn't build it to impress anyone else, though. I built it because I thought it was pretty cool. I also won the science fair in my sophomore and junior years.

My senior project was about dinosaurs. I had been working on it since the tenth grade. I was curious about why dinosaurs in Montana were so different from the dinosaurs found in the same type of land formation in Alberta, Canada. That year, I won first prize at the science fair again. Two years ago, I finally published the answer to the question I was curious about. It took me all that time to find the answer.

Even though I was winning the science fairs, I was still doing poorly in science classes. The teachers wanted us to memorize for tests. I can't even understand what *memorization* is. I don't think it's possible for me to learn; it's just something I can't do.

My grades proved that. I remember getting only one B in my life. The rest were a few C's, mostly D's, and lots and lots and lots of F's. But I always believed in myself. This came from knowing that there were other things that I could do better than anyone else. My science fair successes and most of my successes in my career have come from an "I'm doing it my way" attitude. Finally, I graduated from high school with a D minus in English. My teachers said they would have flunked me, but they didn't want me there again.

I wanted to go to college because there were more books and more stuff to learn about science. I had lots of questions that I wanted to answer. Back then, some colleges accepted you even if you had bad grades, otherwise I couldn't have gone. Throughout college, I learned a lot but I kept flunking out. I still couldn't memorize. It was also hard for me to keep up with lectures. In chemistry, I remember my teacher writing on the board and talking about something else at the same time. I couldn't follow either. And I could never keep up with all the reading.

The college kicked me out for failing, but I kept going back. Then some teachers came to my rescue and said, "We don't know what's wrong with him, but he obviously has the interest. We know he's bright, but he can't seem to get through these classes." I took every undergraduate and graduate course in science that I could find. It took me seven years to do this, but I never got a college degree because I had failed too many classes.

After I had taken every class I wanted to take, I wrote to English-speaking museums all over the world looking for any job related to paleontology. I was offered a job working in a museum in Princeton, New Jersey. At Princeton University, I became a paleontology preparator, which is the person responsible for cleaning and assembling dinosaur bones.

If I hadn't been offered this job, I still would have studied dinosaurs. I knew that I wanted to be someone who contributed something worthwhile to the study of paleontology. And I was hoping I could find something that would help unravel some of the mysteries of dinosaurs. Nothing would stop me from answering the questions I had.

Is memorizing information hard or impossible for you? How do you handle this learning difference? Do your teachers understand?

While I was at the museum in Princeton, I learned about dyslexia and better understood what LD was. I was sort of relieved to understand there was a reason why school was always hard for me, but I had never let my LD stop me from doing what I loved in science.

Whenever I had a vacation, I went right back to the fields in Montana to explore and look for dinosaur fossils. On one of my vacations, my friend and I found something very exciting—nests that contained baby dinosaur bones. This let me know that baby dinosaurs stayed in their nests when they were young. This kind of behavior was unheard of in dinosaurs. It was big news, and lots of people all over the world wanted to know more about it. It took many years to dig up these nests, and we're still digging.

Best School Memory

"Kissing my first girlfriend."

Worst School Memory

"Being caught talking in fifth grade and having to stand in front of the class. I was really embarrassed."

At this site, Jack and other scientists are digging up the bones of a Tyrannosaurus rex.
▶

Eventually, I moved back to Montana so I could be near the fields. I became the curator at the Museum of the Rockies. I also teach at Montana State University in Bozeman. I never make my students memorize for tests. Instead, they have to explain what they know. Now I have an honorary doctorate from the University of Montana in Missoula, which was given to me by the same man who had kicked me out of college when I was younger.

Because I am dyslexic, I believe I offer a different approach to certain subjects. That comes with the way I think. I think differently, and that makes me ask questions differently. That's just the way some of us dyslexics are.

Information comes into my brain all jumbled up. I sort it out the best way I know how, and it may not always be sorted out right. I just line up the thoughts in the order in which I recognize them, until things make sense. When all the thoughts are lined up, I ask an original question. I don't sit around and think harder, I just ask questions differently. Because I'm not able to remember everything, I tend to remember what's most important. Then I can get to the root of a problem, without over complicating things. People tell me I have an interesting perspective.

If I went back to sixth grade, I would probably get the same grades I got then. There's no way I could get higher grades, especially if the teachers still taught me the same way. But even with all my difficulties in school, I always did what I wanted to do. I wanted to be able to do real science. I wanted to be sure that I was asking good scientific questions and that I had the knowledge to try to answer them. I didn't know I could be paid to be a paleontologist, but I worked very hard to be one no matter what.

If you're interested in something, spend time doing it. It doesn't matter what the subject is. Don't worry about what other people say. With science, sometimes there's the stigma of being a nerd. Just don't pay any attention to that. If you're interested in science, do it. I feel good about what I do because it's exciting and fun. If you like what you do, then life is just a wonderful thing.

Jack says that because he thinks differently, he asks questions differently, which has helped him with his career. In what ways has your learning difference helped you?

"Just do it your way and to your satisfaction! Never worry about the expectations of others. Do it for yourself."

Jack

Jack (right) *served as a consultant to Steven Spielberg* (left) *in the making of the movie* Jurassic Park. *Jack's knowledge of dinosaurs helped the movie-makers to create more realistic looking dinosaurs in the film.*

▶

If you are interested in learning more about Dr. John (Jack) R. Horner or his search for dinosaur eggs and nests, visit his website at http://web.mac.com/johnrhorner/Site/Jack_Horner.html, or check out some of his books:

Digging Dinosaurs by John R. Horner and James Gorman (NY: Perennial Library, 1990). Describes Jack's discovery of a new kind of dinosaur, the Maiasaur, which took care of her babies in nests. This was the first nest of baby dinosaurs ever found.

Maia: A Dinosaur Grows Up by John R. Horner and James Gorman, illustrated by Doug Henderson (Philadelphia: Courage Books, 1990). A realistic account of the life of a young dinosaur.

Digging Up Tyrannosaurus Rex by John R. Horner and Don Lessem (NY: Crown Publishers, Inc., 1995). The remarkable story of the discovery of the first complete Tyrannosaurus rex skeleton ever found.

Dinosaurs: Under the Big Sky by Jack Horner (Missoula: Mountain Press, 2001). Describes species of dinosaurs known to have lived in Montana and explains the scientific importance of their bones and skeletons.

Digging Up Dinosaurs with Jack Horner by Jack Horner, illustrated by Robert Rath and Phil Wilson (Helena: Farcountry Press, 2007). Takes kids along on a dig and profiles dinosaurs that once roamed Montana, Colorado, Utah, Wyoming, Idaho, North Dakota, and South Dakota.

WHERE'S JACK NOW?

One of the most important things to me has been teaching and guiding really good graduate students who go on to publish cool stuff, like Mary Schweitzer's work about soft tissue found inside the bone of a T-rex. First, I try to get my students to think out of the box, to think differently. Those of us with dyslexia really understand the idea of thinking differently, because that's what we do. I tell my students not to worry about preconceived ideas, but rather to try to come up with their own ideas. Mary did just that when she found that soft tissue still exists after millions of years. Before Mary, nobody had really looked to see if soft tissue existed because they thought it would be petrified. People couldn't find it because they thought it couldn't be found. This is a good lesson—it shows you have to test things on your own sometimes, instead of accepting what other people say. If I only listened to others when I was a child, I would have ended up thinking that I was lazy or stupid. You have to go out and test the waters yourself.

I've written even more books about dinosaurs. I try to make the computer do my editing, but usually my spelling is so far off that I ask someone else to edit my work. When I write an article

Jack on the set of the movie Jurassic Park.

about my research for a scientific journal, someone will help me get through all the background reading that's required. Reading is the hardest thing I've ever had to do. When I read, it's word by word. If I look at the words too fast, then I really get very confused. I don't use the computer to read to me because there are so many scientific words it can't say correctly. There's so much I'd like to know, I really wish I could read better. I'd be reading all the time.

I recently spoke at a conference about dyslexia. While I was there, I learned more about what dyslexia really is. Since then, I've been analyzing my dyslexia. It's actually very interesting to me to finally figure out which parts of my learning style are really the dyslexic stuff.

One of the problems I've had since I was a kid was in the auditory area. Whenever people said something to me, I always asked them to repeat it, so everyone thought I was partially deaf. My parents kept taking me to get my ears checked, and had the teachers sit me up in front of the class, but it never helped. The real problem was that I just couldn't put all the words together quickly enough. Now I explain to people that I must ask them to repeat stuff once or twice because of the way my brain works. Some people understand and are patient, but others are just as impatient as before I asked them. I find that kind of interesting in itself.

I've been working with people in Dubai to create a dinosaur theme park and museum. That sure has been fun. I'm also working on another dinosaur movie based on a script that I wrote. The best part of my work is helping graduate students and other paleontologists. When you do what you like, it's really cool.

Peggy Jorgensen

Age 41

*Peggy Jorgensen
loves her job teaching
second grade.*

◄

*Peggy has trouble with numbers but loves to read and write. As a
second grade teacher, she wants to make all of her students feel
good about themselves because she recalls what it was like when
her teachers yelled at her for her weakness in math. Peggy lives in
Connecticut.*

Does your teacher or another adult help you see your strong points? Can you name five (or more!) of your strengths?

Peggy as a student in fifth grade.

Have you tried to keep your LD a secret? Why or why not? Who knows about your learning difference?

I love teaching. It is important for me to make the classroom exciting for my students. I want children to believe in themselves and to know that they each have a special talent. If any of my students have trouble with reading, writing, or math, I help them to see their strong points.

I know what it is like to go to school and feel terrible about not understanding something. All through my school years, math was very difficult for me and made me anxious. I remember how badly I felt when the teacher focused on my weakness. The teachers were good at that. I used to think, "Can't you find something good to say about me?"

When it was time for math, I wanted to climb into my desk and hide. I wanted math to just fly by. I couldn't stand the subject, and I couldn't stand the word *arithmetic*. I used to panic, and I remember that I would start to sweat and my heart would beat fast. I knew I was different from other kids because anything dealing with numbers was just harder for me to grasp. I didn't want my friends to know— this was my secret.

Sitting at my desk, I would use any object I could find to help me answer math problems, even my fingers and toes. But the teachers wanted us to memorize everything, even if the objects helped us. The worst memory I have is going up to the chalkboard to do math problems. If I didn't get the answer right, the teacher would say, "Don't you get it? Don't you know what to do next?" In my mind I was yelling back, "No! I don't get it, help me get it, don't put me through this!"

When I went to school, the teachers weren't big on using blocks or other tools that might help us learn. So I had to make little pencil marks on my desk so I could add them up, subtract, or divide. Anything I could *see* helped. When math got tougher, I used these same compensating skills. In high school, I chose math classes that were easier for me, such as geometry. As a teacher, I have a better understanding of kids with math weaknesses because it was so difficult for me.

Math is still difficult for me, but thank goodness for the calculator—the greatest invention in the world! Though I find it harder to teach math than other subjects, I take courses to continue to improve myself. The courses and my students help me realize the importance of using concrete manipulatives such as

Peggy enjoys reading to her second grade class.

blocks, which make it easier for students to grasp abstract concepts. I also use rhythm and dance to teach these concepts.

I am an excellent reading and writing teacher, and I often help other teachers in these areas. In college, my teachers helped me see that I am a strong leader and that I am very good at making people feel good about themselves. I feel that in grade school, very few people pointed out the gifts I had. That's why in my teaching now I'm always trying to find something good in every child and then share what it is. You can't assume kids know this—they need to hear it.

"When you're feeling that you want to just crawl into some bottomless pit, think of your strengths. Think of all the wonderful gifts you've been blessed with, which make you the great person you are. Believe in yourself always! The faith you have in yourself will pave your way to success."

Best School Memory

"Receiving my straight A's report card from my master's program in education and feeling great."

Worst School Memory

"Going up to the chalkboard and having to do long division. I was ridiculed for not understanding it."

Would you like to have someone like Peggy as your teacher? Why? Who is your favorite teacher? How does your teacher help you to learn and to feel good about yourself?

WHERE'S PEGGY NOW?

I am still teaching, but now I'm in a larger classroom. As a teacher in the Learning Resource Center, or library, I have contact with all the students in an elementary school. Their teachers and I plan collaborative units of study to teach researching skills. The children learn how to ask questions, find information, and how to take notes. There are so many ways to report their findings: create a play, a HyperStudio presentation, a video, or a collage. Lately, the children have been using music to help present their research, which is great.

There are many children with learning disabilities in the school, and I'm sensitive to those kids who have reading and comprehension issues. It's wonderful, being a good role model and teaching to all learning styles.

I also tutor kids in reading and writing. One student's parents asked if I could help their daughter in math. I told them that math was not my area of strength, but I would do as much as I could. After a few sessions, I could really relate to what my student was going through—to her, numbers were so abstract and all over the place.

I've noticed that schools have been teaching math differently. Teachers are asking students to reflect on the process they use to get answers. Now many teachers understand that there are different ways to approach a problem. I think this perspective will help tremendously in the teaching of math.

I'm at the age where I'm planning ahead financially, thinking about ways to make more money while I draw on what I enjoy. I decided to go into real estate, and now I have my license. Sometimes I worry about the math needed to be a real estate agent. Then I remember how I taught math in the classroom and the strategies that were effective, such as finding patterns and using music to teach math. I'll draw upon this knowledge if I get stuck. Maybe I'll create a collection of little songs to help me remember certain formulas. By believing in myself, God will help me accomplish what I've set out to achieve: to become a successful real estate agent.

I've always inspired others through encouragement and support. Now it's my turn to reach beyond myself. One must never stop helping, growing, learning, and believing. If you believe, then you can achieve.

Carlos Trápaga

Age 24

◀ *Carlos at home.*

Carlos's strengths are his thinking and speaking skills. He has difficulty with reading, writing, and memorizing. Carlos grew up in Puerto Rico and attends business school in Washington, D.C. He works very hard in school and relies on different support systems to help him succeed.

Carlos says that when he went to a new school in seventh grade, it seemed to him that people thought his LD "was over." Do you think LD is something you can "get over?" Why or why not?

Do you often worry about passing your classes or getting good grades? What can you do to put yourself at ease? Do you talk to your parents, teachers, friends, or anyone else about your worries? What do they say?

Between first grade and my senior year of high school, I went to six different schools. My school years were like being on a roller coaster because of my LD.

In second grade, my grades were horrible and my parents had me tested to find out why. They found out I had LD, but they didn't know enough about it so they sent me to a psychologist instead of a tutor. She used to ask me about my dreams, but I didn't remember them so I had to make them up.

In school, reading was difficult and I was really nervous when we had to read out loud. I think I blocked out fourth and fifth grade from my memory because they were so bad. The only thing I remember about fifth grade was that we had an earthquake during school! After fifth grade, I wasn't in one school for more than two years. Because of my LD, it was difficult to find the right school. During sixth grade, I went to a special school for children with learning differences and did so well that I got into one of the best schools in Puerto Rico for seventh grade.

When I went to the new school I think people thought my LD was over. I was really scared to be in this school because I knew it was hard, and I didn't know how I would handle it. Sure enough, I started failing because there was no help for students with LD. I started dozing off in class because I couldn't understand the teacher. They kicked me out, and I went to another special school in eighth grade.

My schoolwork improved because of all the support I got at my new school, and I was back in a regular school for ninth and tenth grade. At this school, I began to respect the importance of doing homework. I didn't want to arrive in class without my work and give the teacher any reason to think I was a bad student. Though I started working harder, switching schools so much was shameful for me. At times, my dad got very upset because I did so poorly, and he became frustrated. Over the years, his understanding has changed because he's seen how hard I have worked.

By the end of tenth grade, my grades improved and I was being tutored. School was also getting better because I knew everyone, and this school had girls. I loved parties, and it was amazing to feel so popular. However, I was the only one of my brothers not to go to a school called St. John's, one of the best schools in my country.

The Trapaga family on a ski trip (Carlos is second from the left).

A teacher at St. John's named Jorge started tutoring me. He thought I could get in, and prepared me for the entrance exam. I passed on the second try after studying with Jorge all summer long. Going to St. John's was like a turning point for me. The school was extremely difficult, but I was tutored constantly in almost every subject, which helped me to get through. Jorge helped me with everything: he'd break down the steps of math for me, and he taught me how to write papers, which was very hard. My reading was so slow that I could not keep up with the books. Or, I would forget parts of the book because my memory is so weak. Sometimes I would get friends to tell me about the books, or I would watch the movie.

Though I struggled through St. John's, I really loved it. For the first time, I felt good about myself academically. I was really trying, and I was doing all the homework. Sometimes I did my homework at my father's office, which I loved because I started learning more about the business world. During senior year, my grades began to improve, I worked even harder, and I was involved in school activities. Jorge was still tutoring me, and I got help from other tutors, too. I became more responsible about school, and those two years changed my life completely.

How many schools have you gone to as a result of your learning differences? Which school has been the best for you, and why?

Best School Memory

"Graduating from George Washington University, and just knowing that I finished."

Worst School Memory

"Doing so poorly in school when I was younger because the teachers didn't know what my LD was."

Carlos (middle) *poses with two friends from college.*

Now I was ready for college in America, and I went to George Washington University in D.C. The beginning of college was a struggle. I was separated from my friends and family, and that was depressing. The school was so big, and it seemed impersonal after all the help I had received during high school. It took me a while to get used to the system and figure out what I needed.

By sophomore year, things started changing. I met more people, and having friends allowed me to feel better about myself. Also, my friend Ricardo helped me learn how to get what I needed in school. He told me about the importance of getting to know teachers and other people in the class who can help me. Before that, I was uncomfortable asking for special help. But he showed me that I had to communicate with professors and express myself.

I began to use my LD to my advantage, instead of having it work against me. If I needed a time extension because of my slow reading, I would ask for it. Multiple choice tests are horrible for me because I don't read the questions the way the teacher meant them. Many teachers have no idea how hard multiple choice tests are for students with LD. I asked my teachers to give me essay tests instead, and some agreed. On an essay test, I can express myself completely and include all the important facts. Study groups were important, and I got books on tape to help with the reading load. The LD program at George Washington was also very supportive.

I completed college in five years, which was the recommended amount of time for an LD student. I worked all the time, but I learned how I work best and what I need to do to succeed.

Education became more important to me, and I knew that a Master's of Business Administration (M.B.A.) degree would help me in the business world in Puerto Rico. But I was very worried about going to graduate school—I thought that I might fail. School takes a lot of energy out of me because it is so hard. I take much longer to do things than other people. So I constantly worry about passing. Despite this fear, I applied and was accepted to American University's M.B.A. program. I'm in my first year as a part-time student, and it was actually easy to get back into studying. Of course, I am studying all the time, and I sometimes request special help.

Study groups, tutors, a few understanding teachers, and hard work have helped me get off to a great start. With my knowledge, I will one day return home and build something unique that will leave my footprint in Puerto Rican history.

It took Carlos a little longer to finish college than other students in his class, but he did it and feels great. Is college in your future? Do you think you'll continue your education even though school can be difficult for you?

"You have to know yourself. Find your strengths and put them to work for you. No matter what others might say, always look up."

Carlos

WHERE'S CARLOS NOW?

Business school went really well; I loved it. But I don't learn easily in a classroom. It's hard for me to understand the concepts just by reading a book. Fortunately, I was able to work with tutors. The tutors, however, were not the main reason for my success. My ambition drove me to work hard to get what I could from business school. During this time, I also met a special woman who later became my wife.

After I received my MBA, I decided to stay in the States and not go back to Puerto Rico where I had a support network. I sent out about forty resumes, which my wife's father edited. The only offers I got were from banks, so I went into finance. I had never worked in a bank, so I had a lot to learn. After a while, my boss put me on a fast track because he saw I worked hard and had ambition. My job in asset management and investing led me to Latin America, which was really exciting.

There's not a doubt in my mind that my LD affected me every day at work. It's hard for me to read a whole document. I skip around, and it's hard to focus. Sometimes I look for alternative ways to get the information, or I ask someone to read and tell me the important points. Computers are also helpful. I feel comfortable sending emails because the computer corrects my spelling.

Eventually, my wife and I moved back home to Puerto Rico to raise a family. I took a job with the largest bank in Puerto Rico. I was given the job of vice president, sales manager and head of securities, and brokerage services. I was the head of the office, which was a high level position. It really was an achievement. During this time, I also had three children, my biggest accomplishment yet.

Last year I decided to buy a business with my family. I think my parents, who always believed in me, supported this plan because they saw how successful I was. We bought a large food distribution company in Puerto Rico. I became the president, and I am the only member of my family running the business. My learning disability also affects this job—there are things I can't do well, but the things I can do, I do better. When I'm not good at something, there is someone who's been hired to do that job. One of my strengths is that I can talk with people about anything, which is helpful in business. The company is doing well and our sales are up 15% from this time last year.

My approach to life has helped me. I'm ambitious and I never let my learning disability get in the way. I don't talk about it with people at work. I just focus on what I have to do. Though I spend long days in the office, it's my family that really fills me. My incredible wife helps me stay disciplined and encourages me to excel. My daughter is already at the top of her class, doing work in kindergarten that I have to read a few times to digest! I am so proud of my children. I have a very supportive family.

The Grunows: John Jr., April, and John III

Ages 49, 16, and 13

The Grunows: John Jr. (left), *April* (right), *and John III* (front) *at home along the Connecticut shoreline.*

There are actually four members of the Grunow family, including Lisa Grunow (wife and mother). April, John III, and their father have something special in common: they all have LD. The Grunows live in Connecticut.

Best School Memory

"Meeting my wife."

Worst School Memory

"When my Spanish teacher made fun of my test score."

John Jr.

When I was growing up in the 1960s, the teachers didn't know very much about LD. I could tell I was different, because my friends could do a homework assignment on the way to school and know it, but it would take me all night to do the assignment and I still wouldn't know it. This guidance counselor, Mr. Queery, used to take me out of class to find out what was wrong with me. The teachers looked at me as if there was something else bothering me. Of course, there wasn't something else bothering me—it was just that I couldn't learn as fast as everybody else.

It was absolutely impossible for me to learn a foreign language. I can't tell you how many Spanish courses I've taken, and I must have had 25 tutors. The worst thing I remember is my Spanish teacher in high school saying, "The Grunows got 100 percent on the test." My brother Steve had gotten a 90, and I had gotten a 10. Now I have companies in France and would like to know how to speak French for business, but trying to learn the language is pretty impossible for me.

Because the school didn't recognize my language-based LD, I had to learn to cope. I learned street smarts, how to get around the problem. I had to develop a tremendous ability to see the big picture rather than focus on details.

While I'm looking at the big picture, I begin to see how I can make the different pieces fit to my advantage. My vision in the marine industry was to put the best qualities of many small companies into one strong company. This vision turned my company, International Marine, into the largest marine accessory company in the world. Some of the people at school who were getting A's now work for me. My way of learning became a plus, not a handicap.

April

When I was in third grade, I used to come home crying every day. The kids in my class made me feel stupid. They used to say, "Don't you know this, it's so easy." I remember, too, my friend next door always did her homework really quickly. I'd look out the window and see her playing. I'd wonder why

April displays some of her artwork.

I couldn't go outside. But now I am doing so well in school that I hardly remember the bad times I had in third grade.

After third grade, I switched to a school for kids with LD. The classes were small, and I got a lot of help. Now I'm back in a regular school, and my teachers understand that I may have problems learning sometimes.

Like my dad, I had a really hard time learning a foreign language, but because I have LD, I don't have to take a language anymore. I hate taking tests. I have trouble memorizing what I need to know and understanding the test itself. But once someone helps me get started, I can go on. My brother and I both get time extensions on tests.

I really don't care about having LD. I just learn differently from other people. If they have a problem with it, tough. Also, I have many interests outside of school. I love the business world, and I work in my dad's office on the computer.

My artwork and my computer skills have helped me a lot. I love doing landscapes from my imagination. I'm in advanced art classes, and I'm painting a picture of the school for my headmaster as a surprise. I found areas where I can be the smart one. These are my strengths, and I can show them off.

Best School Memory

"Feeling comfortable at my mainstream school—I love it."

Worst School Memory

"When I first went to my mainstream school, and I felt so different because there were more kids, more tests, and everything moved so fast."

John III

John III loves to play tennis and hopes to become a professional tennis player someday.

???

Do you dream of going pro in a certain sport? John has heard that if you really love a game, you have a better chance of becoming a pro. Do you believe this is true?

???

Are you given extra time to complete tests like April and John are? Could time extensions help you? What strategies might help you to complete projects and homework?

In second grade, I hated it when I didn't know what the answer was and everyone else did. The teacher would call on me and I'd think, "Oh no, I hate this." Then, in third grade, I went to a special school like April, and that was a lot easier.

Learning how to read was hard, but math was always one of my easiest subjects. Language and grammar are hard for me—stuff like "subject" and "compound subject" gets annoying to me. It takes me a while to finish tests, and I'm always the last one finished. I get time extensions on tests. Also, cursive writing is hard for me to read. Most of my teachers write in cursive, and it takes me a little while to follow directions written in cursive. I have to read over the sentence to make sure that I know what I'm doing.

I want to be a pro in tennis or hockey. I'd like to be in sports when I get older. I want to be working hard outside, instead of in an office. I was ranked in tennis in New England in the 12-and-under category. They say if you really love the game you have a better chance of becoming a pro, and I really love it. In school, I'm really good at gym and it feels great. If you're not so good in languages, you can be good in sports.

"LD is just a different way to learn. Don't worry if it takes you a little longer than expected or if someone calls you stupid. Believe in yourself and try your best! Your LD will lead you to your strengths in life."

John April John III

WHERE ARE THE GRUNOWS NOW?

John Jr. says:

The marine company I created grew to the point where we had a couple thousand employees and offices all over the world. We supplied accessories to all the major yachts, including those in the America's Cup. My work took me to Australia, New Zealand, France, England . . . all over the world. Flying everywhere to check on operations took me away from my family. After twenty years, one of my friends told me that I was becoming a workaholic. That's when I realized it was time to sell my company and change my life.

I sold the company for more than I expected. Now I have more time to spend

with my family. I'm close to age 60, so I've gone to sort of a partial retirement. I focus on developing real estate in Florida, which I purchased after the sale of the company. I figured that real estate was a good investment. There are more and more people, and God is not making any more land. My learning style gives me a macro approach in terms of investing. I know how to ride through economic slumps, like when interest rates get too high, for the long term. I can still look at the big picture and know that that's the way it goes.

My kids are great. April is doing very well in real estate, and I think her disability became a plus in the way that she interfaces with people. She is such a great people person, and she's using her strength to sell condominiums in New York City. John is learning the real estate business. He also has a macro view about investing. When Apple first came out with the iPod, he understood it was a unique product and suggested we buy stock in the company. The rest is history.

No one in our family used medication for ADHD. I think that some families might be making a mistake putting their kids on Ritalin. Some kids are born with certain traits, like ants in their pants, and that's okay. They should not be medicated so that they become like the cat in the corner of the room. They've got to be able to reach and grow in their own way like they were meant to. I hear teachers talking about these "poor kids" with learning disabilities. Sometimes I can't hold back and I tell them, "You're absolutely wrong. You guys, with a micro view of the world, are the ones that are disadvantaged if you look at people as disabled because they don't fit an exact mold." These so-called disabled people often have a macro view and become industry leaders.

April says:

My grades in high school weren't bad, but my SATs were terrible—I just can't take that type of test at all. Luckily, when I applied to art school, my portfolio was a big part of the application process. I also met the admissions staff so that they could get to know me and see my art instead of judging me on just my test scores. The first art school that I went to was amazing with incredible facilities. I learned so much about the foundations of art. It was intense, though; I often spent all night working on a project and the next day the professor would rip it up and say that it wasn't art.

Seeing my work ripped up every day was just too much, so I transferred to Rollins College. There I had great relationships with all my teachers, who went out of their way to answer questions I had. The art program was nice because I could work independently and then discuss my projects with each teacher. At the first art school, my teachers didn't even know I was in their classes. I realized that relationships are so important to my success in everything I do.

After college I had an internship at the New York Stock Exchange, which helped me to understand I didn't want to be stuck in an office all day. I was always interested in real estate, ever since Monopoly was our favorite family game. So I started studying for my real estate license. I understood the steps of buying and selling apartments so well that I only got one question wrong on the licensing exam. To take the test, I just covered up the answers to the multiple choice questions, figured out the answer on my own, and then found my answer listed each time.

Last year I sold thirteen apartments in New York City. I've saved enough money to start investing in some buildings that I've researched to convert into condos. I'm currently in the middle of three multimillion dollar apartment deals. Part of my success comes from the good relationships I have built with people. Since I can set my own hours, I can also make time to paint in my studio whenever I like. It's nice to be able to do what I do. It never feels like work. I have a smile on my face every day, and I am proud of everything I have done. I'll be working in real estate forever.

John III says:

I moved to Miami for high school. I wasn't tutored in high school; instead, I met my teachers after school for extra help. I did that for math class a lot, where I really struggled. My reading has always been slow and it's still slow. I honestly hate to read. It feels like it takes so long just to get anywhere. In high school and college, I got by through skimming. I figured out how to get what I needed out of the reading. When it came to a test, I don't know why, but I could always remember a couple of random facts to include in an essay. The teacher would often write, "Good comment," and I was happy with that. For me, skimming was better than books on tape.

In college there was a learning center where I went for tutoring and to take my tests untimed. As a political science major, all my tests were essays, which always took me longer to write than my friends. The technology for LD kids helped me tenfold. Some teachers let me use a laptop to type essays for exams, and that helped a lot. For one, my handwriting is pretty awful; for two, I can't spell very well at all. I just can't imagine trying to write a handwritten paper, worrying about grammar or spelling.

It would be great to get into politics, but I'm awful at speeches. That's kind of a minor detail if you want to be a politician! I also like investing. One summer I worked at the New York Stock Exchange. Even though I haven't read many books on my own, I've started reading a book on trading commodities. I might join my dad in his real estate business, which I've been learning about lately. When my dad and I are in the office together, we ask each other the stupidest questions about how to spell certain words. He'll ask me how to spell "pencil" or something. We're both still awful spellers.

I'm also thinking about going to business school. I just don't know how well I can handle the workload, which I hear involves a lot of reading and writing. I think I could learn a lot from business school, I just wonder how well I could keep up. Bottom line, I'm very happy right now, learning the real estate business. I'm getting my Florida real estate license online. In between work, I go deep-sea fishing and play tennis. I'm living in Key Largo and it's great!

David Stafford

Age 14

*David Stafford and his
much used computer.*
▶

David had trouble with reading and continues to have difficulty with writing. He is very strong in science, math, and
computer programming, which is an exceptional talent.
David lives in California.

My parents knew from the time I was very young that I was having trouble with reading and writing. I went to a woman named Nancy White for help. I realized there was a reason that I needed to get help, but I didn't see it as a problem. Nancy got me to the point where I could read and write by the third grade. But I was still behind the other kids.

By fifth grade, my problems in reading and writing started meaning something to me. I couldn't keep up in class because I had to write really slowly for the words to be legible. Because I was a slow reader, it was hard to keep up with longer assignments. But I never had a feeling of inferiority as a result of these problems. That's probably because I am so strong in science and math.

In fifth grade, if I tried to write even close to as fast as I could think, my writing became illegible. My hand just wouldn't move as fast as my mind. If I tried to slow my thoughts down, they would get broken up. I had a problem: Should I think more slowly to keep up with my hand, or try to force my hand to keep up with my mind?

Neither worked. The only other possibility was to get my hand a new tool that would work better. Because I was very interested in computers, I began to use mine for homework. That helped, but I still had trouble keeping up with in-class assignments. I overcame the problem by getting a laptop computer. This opened up a way for me to do good work in class. I can type as fast as I think, get my thoughts down as I have them, and keep up with my work.

Reading was also difficult for me in fifth and sixth grade because we started reading more factual information. I developed strategies on my own and with a learning specialist to read this kind of material. For example, I looked at the illustrations to see if I could understand what was going on. I read the side notes and bold print. Reading the questions at the end of each section also helped.

Then, something happened to me between the summer of seventh and eighth grade. I guess you could say I made a reading leap because I got a lot better at reading. It probably happened because I got into a *Star Wars* book series I really liked, which I kept on reading. The series had a lot of action, and the authors didn't spend the books' first two chapters on character development. Now when I read factual material, I don't have to spend as much time on the strategies because reading has become a lot easier for me.

When do you first remember school being difficult for you?

David as a young boy.

Is there a book or series you loved so much you couldn't stop reading?

At school, David uses his laptop computer in class. ▶

David has found the computer to be a helpful tool. Many people with LD use computers for note taking, writing, rewriting, and checking their spelling. Can you think of ways that a computer might help you? If you don't have a personal computer at home, see if you can use one at your school's media center or library.

I think the main reason I didn't have a serious self-esteem problem about my LD was because my dad was spending time teaching me what I was good at. He started working with me on science and math during second grade. We moved from the basic mathematical operations to pre-algebra when I was in third grade. In fourth grade, I was doing the type of algebra that we're learning in honors math class now.

My math skills led to my interest in science. My dad taught me about atoms and molecules. We made up word problems about force and motion. I was enthusiastic about all of this and still am. My friends and I talk about Albert Einstein, $E = mc^2$ (the theory of relativity), and nuclear energy. Most people know Einstein for $E = mc^2$, but I think he should be known for pondering things like gravity and how space is organized.

My three strongest areas of knowledge are science, math, and computers. By combining my science and math knowledge with my computer skills, I've created a computer program based on the periodic table. My program calculates information about different elements and compounds. I've been able to use it during science tests in school. But my favorite type of programming is game programming. Games require so many different areas of knowledge, such as artistic and programming knowledge. In the future, I'd like to work with a group of people who program games.

Because I understand how computers work, if my laptop breaks I can usually fix it. I really need my laptop because I do all my writing on it. This includes note taking in class. Even with a spell-check program, I still ask my parents to read through my papers for mistakes. I don't think I'll ever be a fast and legible writer, so I really appreciate what using a laptop has done for me.

Best School Memory

"When I got my grades back last semester and they were the best I've ever gotten."

Worst School Memory

"When my laptop was broken for a month in sixth grade."

"Dive into your strengths and forget your weaknesses—this is the best advice I can give. I have found that concentrating on your weaknesses is in vain. You need to wait until your brain is ready."

David

WHERE'S DAVID NOW?

I did really well in high school. I decided not to attend the most prestigious high school I got into because I didn't feel like working as much as that school demanded. Instead, I wanted the freedom to pursue other academic interests, such as teaching myself more electronics and computer science. During my junior year, I built a computerized robot completely from scratch. The robot moved around, crashed into things, and got confused. I entered this project into the Intel Science Fair and got into the semi-finals. It was really cool to get this recognition, and it probably helped me get into college.

High school was relatively easy. I never had any trouble in the mathematics or science classes. My English and social science classes required more effort, which I didn't give them. I didn't turn in work promptly, though the work I did turn in was always of acceptable quality. Because I read so slowly, I'm lazy, and had other things that I wanted to do, I often didn't read the assigned books. It wasn't difficult for me to pick up enough information from class to get by. If I needed to write a paper, I read what I needed specifically for the paper.

I applied to seven universities and they all accepted me. I chose Caltech because I read the biography of a famous scientist, Linus Pauling, who was a professor there. When I visited the school I liked it because the students seemed very, very motivated and interesting.

At Caltech I focused on computer science. College was a lot more challenging than high school. I had to turn in work that was both thoughtful and neatly organized. That took getting used to because I'm not very good at organization and presentation. Also, I took several classes where both the mathematical symbols and grammar were new to me. It was like learning a new language. I found those classes very difficult.

I didn't ask Caltech for accommodations such as extended time. Each professor had his or her own policy about modifications, so it would have been a lot of work to ask. Even so, I never took an exam where I felt I knew the material and could do the work, but ran out of time. There were lots of exams, however, where I felt I didn't know the material very well and was taking forever to finish because I had to figure everything out as I went along.

During college, an employee from Sun Microsystems graded one of my exams and was really excited about one of my answers. Sun then approached me to do an internship, and I went to work there full-time after college. Eventually I left to work for a start-up company. My job is a lot more creative because I'm developing a new computer code. Now, I'm building the building, instead of patching up the foundation.

My LD has a considerable effect on my style at work. I notice that I tend to re-invent things, such as rewriting part of a program. Most people research and then use what already exists. I believe that I rewrite the program because of my aversion to reading. It is often easier for me to write a new program because it's simpler than reading and understanding how to use someone else's.

I may go to grad school one day, but that will depend on many variables like the job market and my job satisfaction. I'm very happy with where I am right now.

Megan Wilson

Age 20

Megan Wilson soaks up the sun at a place called Megan's Bay in the Caribbean.

◄

Megan has difficulty with math, memorization, and spelling. When she went to college in Indiana, she discovered that the services promised for LD students were not available. Megan worked hard to change that and now has the help she needs.

My school history is kind of interesting because I had always been in advanced classes, despite the fact that I have LD. At first, people thought I just wasn't working hard enough when I began having difficulty in middle school. I had problems memorizing vocabulary words and their spelling. Math became very frustrating when I didn't understand the logic behind the numbers.

This was all very confusing because I thought I had the same strengths as the kids in my classes, yet there were certain areas where I could never catch up. Math became so difficult that everyone else went on to algebra and I did

Megan produces a weekly show on her college's radio station. Her show features songs from Broadway musicals.

▶

not. I was trying so hard but was still being told that I wasn't putting forth the effort. After a while, I began to believe this, though at the same time I knew I was studying much more than most of my friends.

In high school, I went to a large school where I didn't receive as much attention. Again, I was in all accelerated classes, including advanced algebra. By the third week, the teacher was convinced that I shouldn't be in the class. That was a big blow, especially because my parents thought that being ahead in math was important.

My other subjects became difficult because I didn't have the rote memorization skills I needed. This affected almost every subject in high school. I didn't understand my memory weakness at the time. I would just study for hours and get C's. At times, I was grounded because my grades were low. Even though I aced anything that had to do with concepts, my struggles with math, spelling, and memorization were too much. My self-esteem started to hit bottom, though I had friends who were understanding and tried to help.

In my junior year, I began to really feel out of place in my advanced classes. My SAT scores were lower than those of my friends, which was embarrassing. I studied all the time, and my grades were still low. Writing essays for exams was awful because the teachers would gripe about my spelling and punctuation errors. Every now and then, I'd get a B in a math or science class and that would be a real reward.

Luckily, one of my teachers went to an Orton Dyslexia Society* conference one weekend. She told me that she thought of me because they described learning patterns that seemed similar to mine. She asked me if I had ever been tested for LD. Though I had heard of learning disabilities, I thought they were comparable to being mentally challenged. Then she mentioned dyslexia, which I knew was associated with people like Thomas Edison. I wanted to be tested right away, since maybe this was the answer to my problems.

Right before I was tested, I went to a youth meeting at an Orton Dyslexia Society conference. I was really nervous, and I was thinking, "What will the students be like?" I walked in, looked around, and everyone looked like me. The students were just like me—smart kids who had the same problems. I can't tell you how amazingly excited I was.

When I was tested and diagnosed with LD, it was the biggest self-esteem boost. This knowledge changed everything and helped to take away some of the frustration. During my senior year, my grades improved because I took classes that better matched my learning style. I went to counseling to help my self-esteem continue to grow, and I met my boyfriend, Dan, who helped me see my special qualities. For the first time in my life, I got straight A's.

I began reading everything I could on LD, and in my senior year, I looked for a college that would offer special help for students with LD. I chose a state university in Indiana because it had a wonderful occupational therapy program and, according to the school manual, it also had an LD specialist and help for students with LD. I knew what I needed, because I'm an independent person and was pretty confident in my skills.

When Megan first heard the term "learning disabilities," she wasn't sure what it meant. Do you remember first hearing the term? Who explained its meaning to you?

When Megan was told she had LD, her self-esteem increased. Why do you think she felt good about her learning differences? Why did she have such low self-esteem before? How's your self-esteem? If it's low, what can you do to raise it?

*In 1997, the Orton Dyslexia Society changed its name to the International Dyslexia Association. For more information, see page 125.

Best School Memory

"A fun snowball fight when college was closed after a 17 inch snowfall."

Worst School Memory

"Preparing for a long time for a test, thinking I did well, then getting a really poor grade on it. That's just a crushing feeling."

However, when I got to the school, I was told that there was no LD specialist, that there would never be one, and that I had to make it on my own. When I tried to question this, the same person told me that if I wasn't happy with the way things were, I might as well leave. This was shocking, and I was enraged. I also knew it was legally wrong. After a lot of crying, I decided that I was going to show him that this was not the way it was supposed to be.

I got to know two other students with LD, and we started meeting with many university officials. We wrote letters to top university officials and top alumni. We presented information about what other universities offered. Along the way, I had teachers who were great about understanding my needs and some who didn't even know what LD was.

It took until my junior year for this conflict to be resolved. The school decided to hire a full-time LD specialist, and asked me to be on the selection committee. We found someone wonderful, and many students now benefit from her assistance. I was finally able to focus on academics, though the struggle to get an LD specialist hired had helped me learn a lot about myself as a person.

Because I understand my learning needs so well, I have been providing myself with special help all along. I get books on tape, have Dan proofread

Megan and her boyfriend, Dan, in front of their college dormitory.

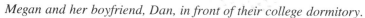

all my papers, and use a note-taking service that has other students take good notes for you. Some classes require heavy memorization, and I make those multisensory. For example, when I had to memorize the bones for anatomy class, I made bones out of clay. I have a cool computer that I can speak into, and my words are then printed out for me.

Because of my experiences, I speak to high school kids with LD about what it's like to be a college student with LD. You have to know what you need and demand it. I'm an optimistic person. Anything can be changed if you put your mind to it.

Megan knew she needed the help of an LD specialist and did all she could to make this happen. What steps can you take to get the help you need?

"No matter what people tell you about how smart you are or who you are, you know in your heart what's good for you better than anyone else. Believe in yourself!" Megan

WHERE'S MEGAN NOW?

In order to achieve my goal of becoming an occupational therapist, I entered an OT program after college. The professors were incredible about helping me with my learning disability because occupational therapists are all about helping people with disabilities! For example, instead of making me take multiple-choice tests that are so hard for me, my anatomy professor let me draw the nerves and muscles and bones on a picture of the human body. When I worked as an OT in the schools, I used my strengths in problem solving and communication skills.

In high school, I used a computer that would listen to my words and type them for me, which was wonderful. As an OT, I still drooled over the field of assistive technology, which uses computers and other devices to help people with disabilities communicate more effectively. So I started bringing assistive technology to some of my students. Soon I was bugging the head of the assistive technology department, asking, "When there's an opening, I would love to apply." Three years later, I got a job there.

In assistive technology, there is even more problem solving and hands-on skill work needed than I used before. Working with students who have complicated problems, I have to think about the technology and what the students need. What are their barriers, and what technology will give them the most independence and success possible? These days, there is even technology which enables a paralyzed person to use a computer.

Recently, I met an amazing kid who is brilliant at math and severely learning disabled. When he came to my evaluation, he was depressed because he knew I would ask him to write, which was such a struggle for him. Finally, I sat him down in front of a program called Word Prediction. This program suggests words after the student types just a few letters. As he began to type, his face just lit up. He was so ecstatic and told me, "It knows what I'm going to write!" Now he's more excited about writing; the technology has made such a difference.

I'm currently taking an advanced level assistive technology course. Dan, who is now my husband, helps me with the really dense reading. He also still proofreads for me. Before any big report goes out, Dan reads it. Sometimes I talk to students about being dyslexic. It's important for kids to see that there are adults who are just like them, making it in the world. When I help kids to use the assistive technology, I share my story with them because I understand how hard it is to learn how to use it. I've been there, and still use it on a daily basis. That extra connection helps me to get kids invested in the technology, because it's not easy.

It's just wonderful when I can open a door for students and see the look on their faces, knowing that they are finally feeling successful.

Samuel R. Delany
Age 54

Writer Samuel R. Delany surrounded by books.

◄

For Samuel, writing was the toughest subject in school. However, he enjoys the written language so much that he became an author of science fiction books. Though he continues to struggle with writing, he has authored over 30 books. He lives and writes in New York City and is also a professor.

How are your dictionary skills? Does it take you a long time to look up words? What techniques do you use?

Not so long ago, educators didn't know much about LD. Many thought bad behavior, not LD, was the explanation for a student's problems. Have you ever been told you had bad behavior when what you really had was LD?

You haven't lived until your sixth grade English teacher has told you to look up in the dictionary every misspelled word in your paper. Think of spending two hours over a large dictionary, looking for the word *running*. I knew it had an *R, U,* and *N* in it, but I didn't know which letter came first.

When I was in school, dyslexia wasn't an acknowledged condition. Everyone knew I was very bright, but still I handed in papers filled with spelling and punctuation mistakes. The errors in my papers were so bad, often people couldn't even read what I was trying to write. The split between my writing ability and my verbal intelligence was diagnosed as "attention-getting behavior." Teachers began to think I was disturbed. When I was 12, I was sent to a psychiatrist. But the problem was not "attention-getting" at all. I was severely dyslexic.

In seventh grade, things came to a head. I was very interested in science. Convinced I would grow up to become a nuclear physicist, I read many children's books about Albert Einstein's theory of relativity. I decided to write a paper on the topic and handed it in to an English teacher I really liked. Because of the unusual subject matter of the paper and all the spelling and punctuation errors, the teacher called me in and said, "Sam, I can't make heads or tails of this. And I don't think you can either. I think you're a very sick little boy!" I had worked so hard on the paper, and I respected the teacher so much, that I was crushed. I ran out into the hall and began to sob. This kind of thing happened often throughout my school years. It was pretty grim.

I did what a lot of kids do when there's a conflict. I blocked it out. When I was made aware of the problem, my response would be to fall to pieces. But five minutes later, I'd get it back together and try to pretend it hadn't happened. Also, I developed a rage to understand difficult things. All I had to do was hear that something was complex, and I wanted to know everything about it.

In middle school, I insisted on doing a book report on Henry James's ghost story "The Turn of the Screw," just because my teacher said it would be too difficult for me. I read T. S. Eliot's *The Waste Land* about 15 times, then started reading books *about* it because I was determined to understand it. All you had to say to me was, "You're too young for this book" and that was the book I'd read next. Because of my early difficulties with grammar, I also began studying grammar books and turned into a "grammar fiend."

Sam and his daughter Iva, who also has dyslexia, spend time together on the day before her graduation from college.

In high school, I read an essay by American writer Gertrude Stein, in which she wrote, "The paragraph is the emotional unit of the English language." A light came on in my head: Change the paragraph when the emotion changes! Discoveries like that helped my own interest in writing to grow.

During high school, I tried writing my own novels and short stories. After high school, I married a woman who was a fine poet and who became an editorial assistant at a publishing company. As a private joke for her, I began to write a science fiction novel. When I showed it to her, she suggested I submit it to her boss. I did and it was accepted. That novel, *The Jewels of Aptor,* was written and sold when I was 19 and published when I was 20. To date, it has sold over 250,000 copies.

I never decided to be a science fiction writer. But after my third science fiction novel was published, I realized, "Oh dear, I must be a science fiction writer." From then on, my goal was to be a *better* science fiction writer.

Best School Memory

"My high school creative writing class and all the people I was friends with there."

Worst School Memory

"The comments my teacher made about my theory of relativity paper."

Sam signs his books for his fans.
▶

When I was 22, my wife read an article about dyslexia and was reminded of me. Because we had gone to high school together, she remembered many of those unpleasant incidents I had tried to forget. Because of my dyslexia, many things that come naturally to others I've had to analyze in great detail to figure out.

While I was writing novels, I also made two attempts at going to college. On the first attempt, I did pretty well my first semester but dropped out during the second semester. Dropping out felt like a failure. I knew I was smart, but in college the organization of my time was beyond me. Also, writing papers for class was just hard. Writing even a simple paper took me five times as long as it did most people. I felt defeated.

After selling four or five novels, I made a stab at going back to college a second time because I really wanted a degree. But I still couldn't juggle my time between schoolwork and writing for a living. My failure with college felt like a failure and still feels like one.

When you write novels, you experience things vividly in your mind. You get hooked on living in your own imaginative world, where everything makes a little more sense and works out a little better. That's easier for me than writing papers in class for a teacher.

Today, I've written over 30 books that have been translated into well over a dozen languages. But writing is still frustrating. The truth is, I'm not a very good writer. But I've made myself into a good *re*writer! My first drafts are dreadful, but I can rework them. Computers are helpful because they make rewriting easier. As a professor at the University of Massachusetts, I tell my students that *everything* has to be rewritten. For me, there is a minimum of four drafts of anything I write.

A novel of mine called *Dhalgren* was republished. The main character is dyslexic and is trying to be a poet at the same time. Actually, dyslexic writers are not rare. Many famous writers, such as Gustave Flaubert and William Butler Yeats, were dyslexic. Yeats didn't learn to read until he was sixteen. Virginia Woolf probably was dyslexic, too.

Dyslexia can be overcome, even for writers. I don't mean you can "cure" it, but you can develop strategies to get around it. Many writers and other people have developed their own strategies, and knowing that has helped me. Though it is very difficult for me, I plan to be writing forever.

Do you enjoy reading science fiction books? What do you know about some of the other authors Sam discusses?

"Go slowly and ask lots and lots of questions, and soon you'll figure out your special way to do it."

Samuel

WHERE'S SAM NOW?

The decade between fifty-five and sixty-five is full of changes. Middle-age is definitely over. At first a kind of a nuisance, arthritis is now more and more a real problem. Suddenly I am buying more condolence cards than birthday cards. On the other hand, for those of us with LD, a dozen to three dozen words I thought I'd never learn to spell more times than not now come out right: "sincerely," "privileged," and "correspondence" usually arrive properly. I wonder from time to time, however, if I'll ever get "occurrence" right on the first try: I'm still as liable to put three "r"s in it as I am to put in one.

The blogs from several young published novelists have called my latest book for Wesleyan University Press, About Writing *(2005), "brilliant," "seriously very, very good" and "the best book about writing I have read in a long, long time."* I still have to do five to twelve drafts of just about everything I write. (Recommendation letters have always been a nightmare and always will be.) From conception to typesetting, About Writing took four years of rereading, rewriting, and polishing. It's funny, but if I didn't have to pay such attention to every detail of the writing process as I do because of my own LD, I probably wouldn't have been able to write a book about the writing process that so many people have found helpful.*

A decade ago I was a Professor of Comparative Literature at the University of Massachusetts. Today I'm an English Professor at Temple University in Philadelphia. Since I live in New York, it's a much easier commute! I teach in a graduate creative writing program, and my manuscript tutorials are a matter of going over the student's manuscript word by word, considering what each word is doing, and how, and why. It's what I've always had to do with my own writing to make it even comprehensible. My students find it helpful in making their own writing better.

My daughter Iva just called to say she's been accepted into medical school (so maybe all that extra work and tutoring and support for her LD when she was a child has actually paid off). Finally, I have learned how to dress warmly enough for winter (yes, layers; but now I seem to know how many layers to put on), and I tend to walk everywhere more slowly—and enjoy the trip more.

Daiana Mozzone
Age 17

Daiana Mozzone, at age 15, is dressed up for her fiesta de quince años, a party to celebrate becoming a woman.

Daiana has difficulty with reading, writing, and following lectures. New information must be very structured for her to understand it. Daiana has tremendous responsibilities at home because she lost her father to cancer. She lives in Florida with her mom and her brother.

Is English your second language? If it is, does this make school more difficult for you?

Do you have an after-school job like Daiana does? Or do you have other activities or hobbies? Do you leave yourself enough time to study?

Though I'm 17, I feel that mentally I am older. I've experienced so much in my life. My dad died of cancer when I was in seventh grade, and that has affected everything. Around that time, I was also diagnosed with LD. I think the reality of how hard life is hit me too early.

My difficulties in school began in first grade. Reading wasn't so easy for me, and I was mixing a lot of English with Spanish when I was speaking. My first grade teacher held me back so he could help improve my reading. That was embarrassing because I was bigger than the other kids, and I felt so stupid. Throughout elementary school, my reading improved a little. And now I'm shorter than most kids!

In sixth grade, a test I took showed that I should be getting help for my reading. I was kind of scared to go into the LD class. I didn't know what happened in those classes. One of my teachers explained that I wasn't stupid, that I had a talent, and that I would come out better after being in the class.

In sixth and seventh grade, I began to understand that my trouble was in reading words and comprehending them. Also, I pick up information in a different way from other people. If a teacher talks too much or jumps from one section to another, I drift off. I have to understand each part from beginning to end.

In the summer before I started seventh grade, my dad was diagnosed with cancer. He was really sick, and my mom had to work to take care of us. Then she would stay up all night to give my dad medicine. My younger brother didn't understand why our dad couldn't play ball with him. My brother and I didn't realize that my father could die. We just thought he'd get better again.

Before he died, my dad gave me his wedding band. He said, "I'm giving you this, and I want you to promise me that you'll graduate." I always think about this promise and how he prayed to live so he could see me graduate.

In eighth grade, I saw how hard my mom was working, so I decided to get a job. Even though my father was gone and there was no man in the house, it didn't mean that someone couldn't pull us through. I worked in a hotel from four till midnight, six days a week, and the money went to my mom.

In school, I did as much as I could, and the teachers were very cooperative with me. But my grades weren't good, and it came to a point where I hardly ever paid any attention to my brother. I started to realize that he would remember

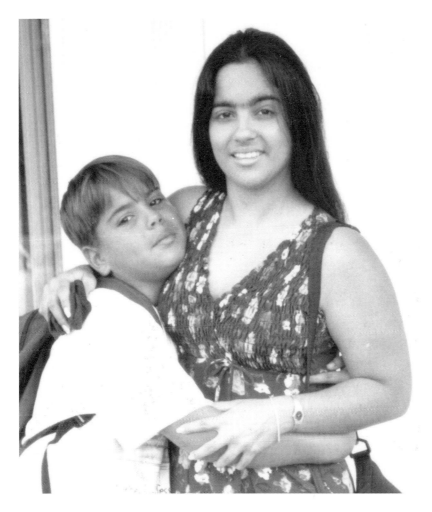

Daiana and her brother, Jonathan.

Best School Memory

"My grades in ninth grade."

Worst School Memory

"Having to go to summer school."

this when he got older. My brother needed to learn that love and respect start in the home and with yourself. So by ninth grade, I quit my job and began to concentrate on my schoolwork.

My LD teacher, Mrs. Sanchez, helped me learn to break down information and to picture it in my mind like a movie. I was doing really well in school and was actually pulling A's and B's during my first year of high school. I also became strict with my brother and made sure he was doing his homework. If he didn't do it, he couldn't ride his bike. Of course, he started doing it.

This year, in the beginning of tenth grade, I got a car and I thought I was cool. I started working again, six days a week. Between school and work, it was

Daiana regrets missing so many math classes, but she feels good about learning from this mistake. Can you recall a time when you turned a mistake into a learning experience?

like a double day. When I got home, I was too tired for homework. I fell behind and I wasn't studying for tests, which was the biggest part of the grade. I started sleeping late in the morning, and then I began skipping school. Finally, I told Mrs. Sanchez that I couldn't keep up and that I was dropping out. She said, "Daiana, either you cut back on your work hours or you're quitting your job, because I'm not letting go of you." I said, "Are you serious?" She's a heck of a teacher because she motivates me and is always there for me, even if I need to study with her at six-thirty in the morning.

While I was skipping school, I noticed my brother started to complain of stomach pains and wanted to stay home. I thought, "He's going to end up where I am now, and he'll suffer." My brother is so nice and sweet, and I knew if he didn't go to school he wouldn't learn new things. I also knew I was letting my father down, and I didn't want that on my back. So I cut back at my job and started doing my schoolwork.

Since that talk with my LD teacher, I haven't missed a day. I've gone from C's and D's on my report card to all B's and one C. Because I missed too many math classes, I have to go to summer school. I slept through those math classes, and now instead of sleeping in all summer, I'm taking math. I regret it, but hey, you know, people learn from their mistakes. Now I know

Daiana helps support her family by working after school.
▶

for my junior year I don't ever want to miss a day. Even if I'm sick, I'm going to school.

I have big plans, and I'm focusing on my life right now. I plan to go to college and get a job that I love. I don't want my LD and other difficulties to get in the way. I'm Hispanic, I can't read that well, and I don't have money-wealth. But I can't let that get to me.

There are two doors in life, just like there's a fork in the road. You can choose any way that you want to go. If one door doesn't open for you, most likely you're going to back up. But I'm saying, "No!" If I have to break down the door, drill a hole, or go through the cracks, I'm going to get through.

Daiana believes that you can always choose your own path in life—do you agree? What path do you want to take in your future?

"Everyone has a difficulty in life—you're not the only one. Some students don't have a positive outlook on life. There's a saying that goes: 'Whether you think you can or you think you can't, you are right.' I'd rather be right by thinking I can."

Daiana

WHERE'S DAIANA NOW?

I dedicated myself to graduating from high school, and I did it. Before I graduated, I learned that ADHD was making school difficult. I also didn't work enough on my reading and writing problems. I was so focused on graduating that I overlooked how important it was to strengthen my English. Ever since graduating, I've been faced with the challenge of communicating by reading or writing, which is so hard. I've learned that I can't ignore my weaknesses, and I'm working on them.

After graduation, I got married and had a baby girl. I was motivated to use my time quickly and learn a skill while she was little. So I went to a trade school for pet grooming. Then I worked in two facilities, learning techniques about handling the animals. I worked hard because I think that whatever you put into this life, you're going to get back.

One day I received a call to buy a grooming business in Delray Beach in Florida. My husband and I owned it for five years. I learned how to use energy, patience, and love with the animals. When I saw a dog come through the door with its tail wagging, I took it as a compliment. Sometimes the dogs would scratch on the door; they couldn't wait to get in.

I developed a clientele of over 800 families. This was amazing, since I'm not college educated, and my reading and writing are not firmly grounded. Sometimes customers asked me to write down a recommended medication. This made me uncomfortable, since I'm not a good speller. I just moved the pen and paper their way and said, "I'll tell you the name of it, you jot it down because I've got to get back to work." My clients would look at me kind of funny, like, why is she getting nervous over this?

In 2005, we closed down and went mobile with the business. I see some clients during the day, and the rest of my time is dedicated to my daughter, who is now in first grade. I have to focus on the educational basics of what she'll need, or she'll feel incomplete. She's learning to read with phonics. Through my daughter, I have a second chance to do schooling again. I can pick up some skills that I'm missing.

By focusing on my strengths as well as my weaknesses, I can enjoy my life and be prepared for challenges or opportunities. I noticed that with my ADHD, sometimes I would get so distracted that without realizing it, I put caring for myself at the end of the list. Meditation has been the only thing that really helps with my ADHD. Meditating helps me to free my mind from worries, to live simply, to give more and expect less. With proper rest, eating, and activity, I have the focus for the next day's journey. You've got to be ready for what life's surprises give you to be able to accept the challenges. The patience and determination I have gained from my academic struggles have allowed me to live according to these beliefs.

Paul Orfalea

Age 48

Paul Orfalea (right) *received an award from former President Bush* (left) *for being an outstanding citizen with LD.*

◀

Paul, who had trouble with every subject in school, is the founder and chairperson of Kinko's, Inc. He had an incredible ability to understand his customers and to give them the services they need. Paul sold his company to FedEx in 2004.

Have you ever tried to cover up that you didn't know something, instead of asking for help? Why? What was the result? Would you do the same thing again?

In second grade, I was in a Catholic school with 40 or 50 kids in my class. We were supposed to learn to read prayers and match letter blocks to the letters in the prayers. By April or May, I still didn't know the alphabet and couldn't read. I memorized the prayers so the nun thought I was reading. Finally, she figured out that I didn't even know my alphabet, and I can remember her expression of total shock that I had gotten all the way through the second grade without her knowing this.

My parents offered my brother and sister $50 to teach me the alphabet, but that didn't work. So I flunked second grade. I had the same nun again, and she was mean. She paddled me for two years, but I still didn't learn the alphabet or how to read.

After that, my mother had me tested everywhere, at this college, that clinic. For two years they thought I couldn't read because I had bad muscles in my eyes. I went to an eye doctor to do eye exercises. Then I went to a speech teacher who thought I had a lazy tongue because I switched my *R*'s and *W*'s.

Paul (standing, far right) *poses with coworkers at his first store in college.*

Every summer, I went to summer school, and during the school year I was in every little special group. I was in the speech group, the corrective posture group, the purple reading group, the green reading group. In third grade, the only word I could read was *the*. I used to keep track of where the group was reading by following from one *the* to the next.

Finally, my mother found a famous remedial reading teacher who knew I needed to learn phonetics and who understood my dyslexia. By seventh and eighth grade, I still had barely learned how to read. I wasn't too worried about it then because I somehow knew I'd have my own business one day, and I figured I'd hire someone to read to me.

My parents never made me feel stupid. They were very nurturing and did not emphasize grades. To them, it was important that I knew something about a subject, could apply this knowledge, and could discuss it intelligently. My best subject was current events, and we were always talking about this at home. I had the perfect parents, which was great because by ninth grade I had flunked again. I never liked the idea of being a double flunky.

By the time I was 15 or 16, I could get by in class with reading. But I could never spell. I was a woodshop major in high school, and my typical report card was two C's, three D's, and an F. I just got used to it.

I always worked after high school, and one job was at my dad's factory. Once, they gave me a job picking orders, which was kind of cool. I really wanted to do this job until somebody said, "Don't let him to do that—he can't even read." That was really devastating, and I actually quit my dad's factory.

When I graduated from high school, I had a 1.2 grade point average. I was eighth from the bottom of my class of 1,500 students. To be honest, I don't even know how seven people got below me.

Everyone in my family and all my parents' friends had their own businesses. So, for me, college was just for fun because I knew I was going to have my own business. In college, I majored in business and "loopholes." I knew who all the easy teachers were. Once, I had to take a literature class in which we had to read 13 books. That's like a lifetime of reading for me! So, to get by, I read *Cliffs Notes* and watched great plays on TV.

In my investment strategies class, my teacher almost failed me because I made so many spelling errors on his tests. When he found out I had LD, he

Paul says that he had very supportive parents. How do your parents show their support?

Best School Memory

"When my professor commented on my 'brilliancy.' "

Worst School Memory

"Oh man, there are so many!"

The branch office of Kinko's in Ventura, California. ▶

Paul got his ideas for a successful business by looking around and seeing what people needed. Are you an entrepreneur, like Paul is? Do you invent things or have creative ideas about helping people? What are your ideas?

announced to the class that I was "on the brink of brilliancy" because he looked at my ideas instead of the spelling. The students were impressed after that, and they thought I saw the world a little differently.

While I was in college, I rented a little garage for $100 a month on the main road of campus, which was the perfect location for my business. I sold notebooks, pens, pencils, and had a small copying machine. I made $1,000 some days.

My reading was still poor and I had no mechanical ability, so I thought that anybody who worked for me could do the job better. I wanted to make sure my employees were happy and that they would continue working for me. I felt that if my coworkers were happy, they'd work harder. The business grew, and I even sent my coworkers into the dorms to sell notebooks and pens. The idea came from seeing the need. The store name, Kinko's, is from the nickname my friends gave me because I have curly hair.

My business continued to expand based on the needs of the customers and the suggestions of my coworkers. We talk to each other, and we give each other ideas. There are now over 1200 Kinko's stores worldwide. The stores that make the most money have the best morale and the happiest customers. I care more about the people who service the machines than the machines themselves.

Though reading is still difficult for me, I do like readers. I like the written language because I like photocopying. I believe in double-spacing, since it helps my business!

Recently, my wife was reading a short story to me, and it was very enjoyable listening to it. It was all about symbolism and clouds. When she was reading, we could stop and talk about what it meant and it was nice. I really wish I was a good reader. I would like to enjoy reading and books. I regret not having that ability. The newspapers are the only thing I read, which I love because I am a current events junkie.

When I talk to college students about all of this, I tell them to work with their strengths, not their weaknesses. If you're not good in reading, do something else. Go where you are strong.

"Trust what you see, rather than what you hear. And don't take life so seriously— just enjoy it." PAUL

For more information on Paul Orfalea, please visit www.paulorfalea.com.

WHERE'S PAUL NOW?

Throughout the 1990s, Kinko's continued to expand. Today, there are more than 1,200 Kinko's locations world-wide. The revenues from the stores top $2 billion annually. In 2004, Kinko's was bought by the FedEx Corporation for $2.4 billion and is now called Kinko's FedEx. I am most proud of the fact that Fortune *magazine named Kinko's one of the best places to work three times in a row. As someone with dyslexia, I could have never predicted I would make my name in what is essentially the "reading business."*

I learned many great lessons from my own struggles, from my dyslexia, my restlessness, and what others call my ADHD or "attention deficit/hyperactivity disorder." (I dislike using the term "deficit"; I don't think it is one.) Doing life alone is not second best, it's impossible. We need other people. We need to know how to talk with them, argue with them, build with them, and introduce ourselves to them. This is only one of the gifts of my "disorders," all of which contributed enormously to the building of both Kinko's and of my life. They propelled me to think differently. My "disabilities" enabled me to focus on the big picture at Kinko's, something I call being "on" your business instead of "in" it.

Though I am no longer involved with Kinko's FedEx, I like to think I didn't retire, instead I have "repurposed" my life. With my cousin and other partners, I started a money management firm called West Coast Asset Management. Our company is performing better than the stock market. Another cousin and I develop real estate through our company, O & S Holdings. We build large commercial properties all over the country.

Equally absorbing—maybe even more so—is the work I now get to do in education. Through the Orfalea Fund and the Orfalea Family Foundation, my wife and I have made grants to educational and mentoring programs. We support programs in the areas of "learning opportunities" (we do not call them "learning disabilities!"). For example, we advocate for Universal Preschool so children entering kindergarten are "ready to learn." And I've taught economics to students at the University of California at Santa Barbara. I teach them new ways to think about investing, how to present their ideas verbally, and how to talk with people from "authority figures" to each other.

From my point of view, straight-A types unaccustomed to failure enter the marketplace and take their first belly flops especially hard. They're so shocked they don't know how to react. That's because our schools are producing test takers, not creative thinkers. Also, what we really want to produce in our kids is resilience. With so much emphasis on high SAT scores and 4.0 grade point averages, I think our schools and universities are selecting out the resilient kids, eliminating kids like me. Some kids just aren't ever going to grasp the Pythagorean theorem. But they shouldn't be stigmatized for the rest of their lives. Do we really want to learn how to do well on multiple choice tests? Or do we want to do well in life?

Eileen Davidson

Age 10

Eileen Davidson at home in her bedroom, wearing her skating medals.

◀

Eileen has trouble with math and language arts but loves social studies and science. She lives in Massachusetts, where she is a figure skater. Eileen skates solo and is also a member of a synchronized skating team.

Do you feel embarrassed to tell your teacher when you don't understand something? Why or why not?

Best School Memory

"Writing my first book at my new school."

Worst School Memory

"When I was embarrassed because I didn't know my three times table in math."

At the skating rink, Eileen shows off her moves.
▶

In first and second grade, I remember that learning how to read was hard. Other kids were reading different books, and I had an easier book than everybody else. I thought I was kind of stupid and that I couldn't learn anything. I didn't tell anybody because I was afraid they would laugh. Back then, my favorite school day was Thursday, because it was a half day.

I would ask my mom, "Why is everybody else on a different book than me? Why am I on a lower book?" She would say, "Oh, it's just because you learn differently." That made me feel a little better.

I started skating when I was four or five. Skating helped me feel better about school. If we had a test and I got an F, I'd go skating and it would make me cheerful. On the ice, it feels like you can do anything. Even if you can't do a jump, it feels like you can. In competitions, it's fun to have everybody's eyes on you. You get all the attention.

School got really hard in third grade. It seemed that lots of kids were actually smarter than me, and the school didn't teach me as much. A woman would come to our class and call my name, and I would go with her. She helped me with reading, math, everything.

In math, I sometimes felt embarrassed and didn't want to go in front of the class and say I didn't understand something. Once, when I did that, some kids laughed but I just ignored them. It didn't feel good, but you should have the courage to go up and tell your teacher you're having trouble. If we had a test and I was scared, I'd think about what my skating coach says: "Try your hardest." And I would.

At the end of third grade, I had barely even gotten up to the three times table. Right after the day we learned it, my mom said, "Honey, you haven't been learning as much, maybe you should go to a new school." And I said "sure." I remember telling my friends, "I'm going to a new school, and I'm going to miss you!" Back then, I wouldn't have told them I have LD because I didn't understand what it was. Now my friends know. They squeezed me until all the information came out. They don't care, and we're all still friends.

For the first couple of months at my new school, I felt kind of shy but I wanted to learn. Soon I felt like I knew everybody and that I could do stuff. I was excited because the classes were so much smaller, and I thought I would learn a lot more.

At the Carroll school, we don't just spend one day on something. For example, we worked on the nine times table for a whole week, and I learned it. Also, the teachers talk in a different way to teach you. They explain things more, and I learn best that way. My reading is better, but it's still hard for me to read words that are really long—you know, the ones that seem about 500 letters long. Math and language are the hardest for me; social studies and science are my favorites.

In class, I don't really think as much about skating anymore because I know I'm getting better at school. After school, I skate solo and I'm also on a team called the Ice Cubes. I like being on the team. If I fall, people help me get up. Our team has traveled all over the country.

I'm trying to get better in solo skating. I've been working on my axel jump. I practice and practice, but I still haven't landed it. I get frustrated because I have to do it over and over, but I keep trying. I'll keep going until I get it.

One day, I might want to try another school so I can see if I've learned as much as I'm supposed to. If my next school is hard, I hope I can get a tutor. In high school, I want to be able to do the work on my own.

I'm also going to keep skating. I'll practice as much as I can, so I can become a professional figure skater. That would mean being in a lot of competitions and maybe even the Olympics. Before my jumps, I'll be telling myself, "Try your hardest." When I land them, I'll think, "I did it!"

Eileen and her brother, Jim, when they were younger.

Whenever Eileen is in a tough situation, she remembers her coach's words: "Try your hardest." What do you tell yourself when facing a challenge?

"It's OK to have a tutor because they are fun, and you'll learn a lot more. And it's OK to have LD." Eileen

WHERE'S EILEEN NOW?

After skating and competing for ten years, I left the sport at age fourteen. With skating, I had no social life, really. I was always at the rink on weekends. I wanted to have that feeling of being a kid, going to school dances and trying new things. Though I miss skating, I was able to try new activities and hang out with my friends.

In college, I socialized a lot during my freshman year. I was afraid that if I didn't go out, I'd miss something fun. All that socializing hurt my grades. Now in my sophomore year, I want to get better grades, so I'm not partying as much. I spend most of my time in the library. During exam week, the library was open 24 hours a day. I was in my little nook studying, and it was wonderful. The only time I returned to my dorm room was for an occasional shower. I got my best grades, too, and broke a 3.0 GPA. I don't think a lot of kids realize that you can still be social and do your work. But you will feel so much better if you get really good grades than you would if you don't do any work and you're just a party animal.

My best grade was in English class. I've gotten A's for my journal entries, and I love my writing. I can read very well, sometimes it just takes longer. If I come to a word I've never seen I have to slow down, break it up, and pronounce it slowly. If I read too quickly I mess up, so I don't like reading in front of people. I'm still not good with numbers, and I don't think I ever will be. I try my hardest to avoid science classes where I have to use formulas. I'm not good at spelling, either.

I've come to terms with my LD. It doesn't bother me anymore. When I was younger, I was always afraid that people wouldn't understand my LD, and they really didn't. Now I tell my friends that I went to a school for dyslexic kids and that I have learning disabilities. One of my really good friends also went to a school for dyslexic kids. We joke about it all the time. We play cards, and when we total our scores we both have to count on our fingers.

I stopped seeing a tutor when I got into high school. I wanted to see if I could do the work on my own. And I could! In college, if I need help, I ask my teachers to meet with me. When it comes to papers, I have my friends proofread my work. I like the feeling of being independent and not needing the help of a tutor. I guess I want to prove to my parents, and mostly to myself, that I can do difficult work all on my own.

When I was still in high school, I got into painting, and I still paint. Now, in college, I'm pretty sure I'm going to major in art history. I would love to be an art or kindergarten teacher. I love little kids. I love the feeling of having kids look up to me.

At the beginning of my education, I wish I had somebody who I could have gone to, to express more about the feeling of "why can't I read, what's wrong with me." My parents told me that some people learn differently, but your parents are supposed to give you that kind of advice. It would have been nice to have had a teacher who was kind of understanding.

Gavin Dobson

Age 21

Gavin Dobson, hard at work in the insurance business.

Gavin has difficulty with many academic subjects. But when he found the right school, he excelled. After a year of college, he decided he would learn more by working in the insurance business. Gavin left college and is now successfully employed in New York City.

Have you seen someone being made fun of for needing extra help? Has anyone ever made fun of you for needing help? How do you handle this kind of situation?

Best School Memory

"Winning the Peter Gow Junior Award my senior year."

Worst School Memory

"There were so many."

I remember that from kindergarten until the tenth grade, school was difficult for me. I didn't like school, and I didn't want to be there. It felt like the only good reason for going was to see my friends.

In second grade, I wasn't reading at all and I couldn't learn cursive. I was tested, and it came out that I have LD. I had to go to a special reading class, which was embarrassing. My parents tried to comfort me by telling me that I was special. But I didn't want to be special. I wanted to be like the other kids.

The worst was third grade. I had to go to the resource room, and I didn't think it was fair. One day, I ran away from school because I didn't want to go to the resource room. My mother was really understanding, but the principal was not. He paddled me for it, and of course I never ran away again.

We moved when I was in fourth grade, and I was hoping that with the move we could forget about my needing special help. But at my new school, the resource room didn't bother me one bit because of my teacher, Mrs. Morris. She was just unbelievable, and I love her to this day. She'd go out of her way at any moment to help me and anybody else.

Reading began to make sense to me in fourth grade. I saw how the sounds could be the same in different words, and that meant I could read more words. I still read very slowly.

At that time, I began to have a lot of trouble with math. We had timed quizzes. When I saw the timer, I thought that I'd never finish, and before I knew it, the time was gone. In fifth and sixth grade, I was in the lower class for math and reading. I think it's totally wrong to split kids up like that. If you do, they'll stay in those classes right through high school.

In seventh and eighth grade, the resource room was horrible. People called it the "retard room." I didn't want anyone to know I was going there. I'd use a side entrance so people wouldn't see me go in. At that age, you really worry about what other people think of you. You don't want to, but you do.

I was also in all the lowest classes again, and math became an even bigger problem. Because I was in the resource room during middle school, I couldn't be in chorus or take an instrument. I was never in any of the Christmas shows, and I really wanted to be in them. Instead, I decided to run for student council because I thought it would be great to represent our class. I called kids up and asked them to vote for me, and I won. Speaking with people was my strength, and it's really the only way I got through school.

I went to a small school in ninth and tenth grade, where my parents thought I'd get more attention. I didn't want to leave my friends, but I just accepted it. It seemed that I always had to do something different from everybody else. In my new school, there was a room where everyone could go for help. The classes were divided into groups, and again I was in the lowest for all of them. I started getting in trouble in class because I never kept my mouth shut and was always goofing around.

I felt that if I goofed around and tried not to succeed, then when I didn't, my failure was expected. But if I went to class and tried really hard and got a D, I would feel stupid. If I didn't try and I got a D, then I didn't care. Everyone knew I was goofing around, and they knew I didn't try.

I got two D's in ninth grade, which was totally unacceptable to my parents. After I'd finished tenth grade, my parents decided I should go to boarding school. They let me pick the one I wanted, and I picked Gow—a school for students with LD. There was nothing to do at Gow but work. When I look back now, I think that was such a great thing for me because if I wasn't forced, I was not going to do the work.

I learned more about my learning style at Gow. I learn kinesthetically, which means that I have to see it, hear it, and do it to learn it. My grades improved, I made the National Honor Society, and I was getting respect from my teachers. I was Student Body President my senior year and captain of three athletic teams. I put in lots of effort at Gow because I thought, "If this doesn't work, what will?" People talked to me like I was intelligent, and I didn't want that to change. At graduation, I won the highest award that is given for the person who contributes most to the growth of the school.

I received an academic scholarship to attend college. When I got there, I asked myself, "Why am I here? Why am I learning trigonometry when I'm never going to use it and I'm going to forget it in a day?" The social aspect of school kept me there two semesters, but I had no desire to sit in class, listen to a teacher, and get tested. My grades were fine, but I didn't want to be there. I wanted to be out in the real world.

Gavin at his high school graduation.

Do you ever goof around in class like Gavin did because the work seems too hard? What else could you do instead?

What do you think of Gavin's decision to quit college and join the workforce? Would you feel comfortable making this kind of choice? Is there a certain job or career path you might pursue?

I wanted to experience life and to learn for myself. If that meant I'd fall flat on my face, then I would. But I have the ability to cope with pretty much whatever happens. I know how to interact with people, and I have a strong desire to succeed. I had a fear that I just couldn't do school, but I had no fear that I couldn't handle life. I decided to leave school and find a job.

I had grown up around the insurance business, so I eventually applied for a job in an insurance

Gavin enjoys the excitement of working near Times Square.

company. Six or seven interviews later, I got the position after stressing that I was a hard worker and would learn the job. My responsibilities include determining the costs and terms of insurance policies.

At first, I was scared, but because I was scared I worked harder. Now I've been there over a year and a half, and it's great. All I hear from my boss is how happy everyone is with my performance.

My LD affects me at work the way it affected me at school. I take a while to read, and if I have to, I work late and on the weekends to catch up. I use a calculator, but I also understand the mathematical concepts that I'm using each day. At night, I take insurance classes. The next day, I see how what I've learned works.

Of course, there are hard days and the work gets demanding. But at the end of the day, I have the best feeling of accomplishment. Every once in a while, when I'm walking through Times Square, I stop and think, "Wow, I work here. It's exciting, and I'm proud of it. I'm doing exactly what I wanted to do."

"Believe in yourself and your strengths, because you can do anything."

Gavin

WHERE'S GAVIN NOW?

My life, which is always an adventure, has changed in so many ways that it's hard to keep track of them all. I changed jobs over five times; in fact, I have started or have been a partner in starting four businesses with varying successes. If something does not completely take control of my senses and engage me, I'm going to want to do something else. So I do.

To advance at my first job, AIG, I figured I needed a college degree. College turned out to be a complete disaster, though. I didn't really think about what it would take to do well, and I didn't put much effort into school. I only briefly looked into the disability services offered. Every once in a while, I tell myself that I'm not learning disabled, and I can do the work on my own. I'm not too successful when I do that. Basically, college just wasn't for me.

For a while I ran a software company with my father. I headed up the sales department, as well as the support and service department. I've learned that I have a tremendous aptitude for business. I rely on the strength that helped me in school: my ability to communicate with people. Our company was so successful that I was able to move to North Carolina without worrying about an income. Of course I've made mistakes along the way, too. I've taken a lot of knocks, both in school and in life. When I make mistakes, I fix them and learn from them.

I can see business opportunities from a mile away, but the nitty-gritty of starting the business is the hard part. Recently, I started my own business supplying laptops to schools. I'm excited about it because I love sales. You talk to people and initially they're going to say, "no," but you have an opportunity to present the facts and try to change their minds.

My learning style affects everything I do. I have to come to embrace my strengths, such as my communication skills, and face my weaknesses. It takes me longer to read than most people, so I have to allow more time to read and comprehend. I may not have finished college, but it wasn't because I didn't want to work hard. Everything in life is about working hard, whether you choose school or you choose to go directly to work. My parents taught me that life is a long distance race, not a sprint. A positive attitude helps me as I make my own way in that race.

Pat Buckley Moss
Age 62

Artist Pat Buckley Moss in her studio. ▶

Pat Buckley Moss has trouble with reading and writing. When she was a child, she couldn't read and write, but she was very good at drawing pictures. She developed this talent and now is an artist whose work is known worldwide. She lives and paints in Virginia and Florida.

When I was young, I loved the forest. About the forest I could learn. About the trees I could learn. Building a swing or a treehouse was something else I could do. But I believed that as far as schoolwork went, I was dumb, because that's what the adults said.

Though it is ridiculous, I never believed that I couldn't live with Tarzan in the forest and be the best. It would have been fun because I wouldn't have had to go to school. No one would be saying, "You can't do this, and you can't do that," like they did at my school.

School was hard, and I was always standing in the corner. On report card day, I used to never want to come home. I would walk home through the woods thinking, "OK, Tarzan, come and get me now." And I believed that he would. When my mother saw my report card, she would be very mad, and she called me an "impossible child." After this, I'd go back to the woods and play.

In grammar school (the first eight grades), I knew I was different. I was often daydreaming or trying to get someone to laugh and talk with me. I wasn't doing my work, probably because I could not read. I didn't know why I could not read or write like the others. I just took it for granted that I was dumb because that's what I was told.

Have you ever created a fantasy world to help you escape from your problems? Did it help? Do you have other ways of escaping your problems?

Pat (left) and her sister, Mary, as young girls.
◀

Do you sometimes feel that you frustrate or disappoint people? If yes, why do you feel that way?

My aunt tried to teach me to read after school. I hated that because I had trouble with reading in school, then had to do it after school, too. It really was awful for me because I knew I was going to disappoint her. I tried to memorize what she was saying, but I said the wrong words. She'd be tearing her hair out, saying, "What am I going to do with you?"

My writing was illegible, and I made it that way on purpose because I could not spell anything. I could make a *B* look like an *E,* and who was to say what that letter was? At home, my mother told me to stop daydreaming while I was in school. But daydreaming was a way to have fun since I couldn't read.

Because I couldn't read, I concentrated on what I *could* do. While everyone sat at the kitchen table and did homework, I would draw. I told my parents that I didn't have homework, even if I did. Instead, I looked out the window and drew the tree and the squirrels. I may have been a dunce at the written word, but I could tell stories through my drawings and get lost in the pictures. Art was a place for me to go. The aunt who tried to teach me to read gave me a watercolor pad and watercolors for my birthday one year. I thought, "Wow, she really believes in me."

My grandfather was the one who really encouraged me. He never let me feel that my problems were of my own making, and I could talk to him like a real friend. He made me truly believe that if I wanted to do something and tried my hardest, I would succeed.

Throughout grammar school, I just lived in my imagination. I passed each grade only because I was a big kid and the teachers kept pushing me on. Once, a teacher was reading a composition out loud and all the kids were laughing. So I started to listen, thinking that the paper had to be a funny one. The teacher was saying, "And this word is spelled wrong, and this grammar is wrong, and that is wrong. And Patricia Buckley, this is yours and you should be ashamed of this paper." It was very mortifying because now the whole class knew I was dumb.

I remember on tests I would get about four right out of twenty. I don't remember ever getting a good grade on a written paper—ever, ever, ever. The only good papers I ever got were drawing papers, and the teacher would tell my mother, "Well, she can draw, and you've got to concentrate on that."

When it came time for high school, a wonderful teacher urged my mother to find me special training so that my talent as an artist would not go to waste.

What do you think of the teacher who read Pat's paper out loud to the class? Have you ever been laughed at because of a mistake you made in class?

I was accepted to a high school in Manhattan that specialized in the arts. In this school, I was taking four periods of art a day and wasn't called a dummy. We were all treated with respect and could see that there was a future for each of us. Art became more and more important to me.

While I was in high school, I learned about a college called Cooper Union. This was a school designed for artists and scientists, which meant it had as much respect for artists as it did for scientists. This was very, very exciting, and I thought the school sounded like a wonderful place to go. I was actually accepted, which was surprising to me because some of the smart students weren't even on the waiting list.

Cooper Union turned out to be everything that I had hoped for. From my very first day, I was aware of the atmosphere of professionalism among our teachers, and that inspired the students. However, I did feel that they were going to find out that I was stupid and kick me out. I was absolutely worried about that. Isn't that wild? It's a terrible way to live.

Fortunately, the school supported you in any way, as long as they knew you were really working hard and enjoying what you were doing. They let me write the way I wrote, without periods or question marks. I used a lot of dashes, a more free-form style of writing. In my art history classes, the lectures contained the information that was also in the books, so I had a way to learn the material. Some of my teachers gave me tests orally. I just loved everything I did

Best School Memory
"In an assembly, I was surprised because I was called up for an art award."

Worst School Memory
"When the teacher read my composition out loud and everybody laughed."

In a classroom of kids with LD, Pat works with students and shares stories of her struggles in school.

Pat talks about being labeled as a child. Has this happened to you? Why do you think people label others?

at the school, from etching and calligraphy to painting and drawing. I knew I was going to draw pictures for the rest of my life because art was what I could do.

After college, I got married and raised a family of six children. I continued to paint because I loved it, but I never thought about making money with it. I painted religious scenes, natural scenes, and the sweetness of the Amish people. I joined a local art group and entered a few pieces in a show. My paintings won in the category of watercolor and oil, and I was given a one-person show. It was really neat—I filled three rooms with paintings and sold almost every piece. People were buying everything, and I thought, "Wow, you can make money with this."

I started showing my work out of town and would often sell every piece. Now, that was terrific—doing what I loved and making money at it. More and more people became interested in my work, and it began to appear in galleries all over the country.

Around the time I was 45, I heard a program on the radio about dyslexia. I remember thinking, "Oh, my! I was like that, I did that, that's the way it was, that's the way it happened." When you're not helped as a child, and you're labeled, I think it's very hard to get rid of the label. I know I'm not dumb, but at times I remember that "dumb" is what I was called. It's a strange thing.

Now I speak to kids with learning problems in schools all over the country. I understand these children because I was one of them. I encourage them to find something they love and work very hard at it. I continue to work very hard at my art, and I'm working all the time. All kinds of people respond to my artwork, and I've been called "The People's Artist." Painting in the quiet and peace of my studio is something I love. Creating strong, bold trees or beautiful flowers is divine. It's like making your own music, and every day is absolutely wonderful.

"Like what you do in life, do it the best you can every day, and be honest about it."

Pat loves to draw trees, as seen in her painting Winter Serenade.

If you want to learn more about Pat Buckley Moss and see her artwork, you can look at her book or video, visit her museum, or check out her website:

P. Buckley Moss: The People's Artist by Pat Buckley Moss (Waynesboro, VA: Shenandoah Heritage Publishing Company, 1989). This autobiography tells about Pat's life as an artist and her struggle with dyslexia. The book is available through the Moss Portfolio. Call toll-free (800) 430-1320.

"Split the Wind" is a videotape about Pat's life, art, and struggle with dyslexia. It also offers a mini tour of the P. Buckley Moss Museum. The video is available through the Moss Portfolio. Call toll-free (800) 430-1320.

The P. Buckley Moss Museum is located in Waynesboro, Virginia. For more information, call (800) 343-8643.

The P. Buckley Moss website (www.pbuckleymoss.com) includes a biography of Pat, a collection of newsletters describing her latest activities, and a list of galleries where you can see her artwork.

WHERE'S PAT NOW?

Everything is a learning thing in this life, and I'm still growing. My art continues to be refined. I wake up and I can hardly wait to get to my drawing board.

I've just finished a second piece of art about 9-11 called "To Our Heroes." It includes a search and rescue police dog; I think it's a great piece. The dog is just so intelligent and beautiful looking, the way he looks at you with the destruction behind him.

In the last ten years, I took a break from showing, but now I'm back. It's been great returning to galleries and seeing dealers who are friends. The input from people about my art has truly been very good.

Though I'm older (I really don't know that I'm older) and have to take things at a slower pace, I still give talks to teachers. I tell about my life and my experiences in school. It's wonderful that more kids are getting help, but not all kids are yet. There's still a need to help teachers know how to identify children with learning differences, and not to put children down if they have a problem. The most important thing is to treat children with respect instead of intimidating them. We have an art program at our museum for children from needy families. Through art, we work with the children to build their self-esteem. It's wonderful.

I still love what I'm doing. No matter what it is that you do, it's great when you enjoy what you do in life.

"To Our Heroes" by P. Buckley Moss, 2006.

Robert Rosenberg

Age 18

Robert Rosenberg in his bedroom, with his sports awards on the wall behind him.

◀

Robert is very sociable, an accomplished athlete, and a strong thinker. But he has trouble with writing, organizational skills, and paying attention. He lives in New York and plans to attend the University of Michigan.

Think of a goal that you have reached and all the steps it took you to get there. How did you feel at the moment you reached it? How do you feel when you think about it now?

Best School Memory

"Being elected Student Body President."

Worst School Memory

"When I was reading out loud and another student filled in the word when I paused to figure it out."

In my senior year, I was elected Student Body President and was accepted to the University of Michigan early decision. This means that I knew early in senior year where I would be going to college. I wasn't expecting all of these amazing things to happen, but they did. Even though I've been working hard in school, it took until my senior year for me to fully feel that I could achieve a lot. As long as I can remember, I have received help from tutors and my parents for my LD. School was a struggle, and having ADD (Attention Deficit Disorder) made it even harder.

I went to an elementary school that was very competitive. I tried to hide my LD. I didn't want people to know, and I tried to avoid reading out loud. I didn't want people to look at me differently.

I guess maybe I didn't exactly understand what LD was and how it could affect me. I knew that the ADD made it hard for me to focus and that I had so much energy. I had so many tutors, and my mom helped me with all my work. I got help with everything—English, math, grammar, everything! I also remember my friends saying, "Oh, wow, that's so simple," and I was thinking, "What are you talking about? This makes no sense."

In the summer after sixth grade, I saw a bunch of applications for other schools in my parents' room. I had no clue they were applying to other schools for me. My entire life, since preschool, had been one school. I didn't know any other schools. I panicked, and was crying and screaming. I thought that my life was ending.

I was hesitant to tell my friends. When I did, I told them I was switching schools because my parents were making me. At that age, you don't want to feel different. I felt like I should avoid it, hide it, run from it. Later, in high school, I was able to tell my old friends that I had switched because of my LD and my ADD.

When I got to my new school, I was in a program for students with LD. I went to regular classes like everyone else and received help in school every day at the Learning Resource Center (LRC). My LRC teacher helped to explain what my LD/ADD was and how I could cope with it. I needed someone to take me through my work so that I could eventually do it on my own—not to do it for me like my old tutors. My LRC teacher showed me how to slow down, because I used to jump from subject to subject and feel overwhelmed. The LRC taught me how to be organized, and now I have organizers and plan books. I can plan ahead, but I still think I do some of my best work under pressure.

During high school, sports helped me develop confidence. When I was in eighth grade, I was invited to join the high school varsity wrestling team. After a very successful season, I wanted more, so I started playing soccer. When I wanted to prove to myself that I could be even better, I moved to track. Sports taught me that perseverance has rewards and that I should never give up if I want to attain my goals.

Being elected Student Body President was the final thing that proved to me that I was really someone. I was not a quitter, I was a doer. My whole school decided that yes, I'm someone they wanted to lead them, to speak for them, to be their voice. It proved to me that I had succeeded and that I had not taken the easy road.

The icing on the cake came when I was accepted to the University of Michigan. Five years ago, if you had told anyone that I would be attending one of the best universities in the country, they would have laughed out loud! I proved them wrong.

Is organization one of your strengths or weaknesses? How do you organize yourself?

Robert (far right) *and his family at home.*

Do you think you could be in a leadership role? Why or why not? Think about some great leaders and what you admire about them.

Wrestling is just one sport Robert (right) excelled at in school. ▶

Do you do as much work as you can on your own before getting help? Do you have a tutor or someone else helping you?

Over the years, my LRC teachers helped me. They really helped me to organize projects and my notes. It's hard for me to be organized. I have time extensions on exams and that helps.

But one thing I want to stress is that it doesn't help to have people do your work for you. I wanted to succeed to prove to myself that I could. Now that I'm going to the University of Michigan, I'm going to see if I can be organized. I've never really done it all on my own.

At Michigan, if you need help they have assistance. But you have to go get it—they don't come looking for you. I work best when there's competition, because I need the push. Michigan is my next challenge, and I'm anxiously awaiting it.

"Don't feel that you are any different from anyone else because you have LD. You can be whatever you wish to be, if only you reach out for the knowledge that lies ahead and grab it with both hands."

Robert

WHERE'S ROBERT NOW?

Columbia Prep was a turning point. There I began to understand my learning disability and how to manage it. At the University of Michigan, I learned about independence and responsibility through hard lessons. During my first semester at Michigan, the organizational and learning skills that I developed while at Columbia Prep went out the door. I waited until a few days before a paper was due to begin working on it and crammed for many of my exams. I socialized more than I studied, and my GPA suffered.

After I received my grades, I realized that I needed to drastically change my ways and apply what I learned in high school. I became more organized and started papers when they were assigned. My roommate edited my papers after he learned about my LD. When I had questions, I met with my professors. When needed, I arranged for extra time on exams and papers, and sometimes took exams in a smaller room. Eventually, I turned everything around, including my GPA.

Sometimes, despite all the hard work, the results were less than stellar. Math and science classes were challenging. I used school resources to find tutors and worked in study groups. Overall, I viewed college as a launching pad for the education I really wanted: law school. During senior year at Michigan, I started preparing for the LSAT. Some sections were easy, while others were extremely difficult due to my disabilities. A tutor helped me prepare and taught me tricks for the tougher sections. I did well and was accepted to my first choice, Brooklyn Law School.

Law school was a new challenge. There were many sleepless nights as I tried to finish all the reading that was expected. At times I was not 100% prepared because I simply could not finish the reading. Eventually I learned how to work with my disabilities to meet the expectations. Some professors didn't mind, for example, when students used condensed reading sources. What I found most helpful was that the professors were so accessible. The most difficult obstacle was learning to write like a lawyer. It took until my third year in law school to feel comfortable with this type of writing.

I married Emily Gelb, a remarkable woman who also grew up with learning disabilities. She obtained a master's degree and now teaches children with learning disabilities. I am so lucky to have found someone who understands LD. I love her so much and am proud of her.

Sometimes I wonder, and I think it's natural to wonder, whether my disabilities limited me. Maybe different doors might have opened for me. But it's not worth dwelling on because I love who I am and the life I have. I graduated from college and law school. I passed the New York State Bar Exam and practice law in New York. I have accomplished so much already, and the story of my life has only just begun.

Lucia Trimbur

Age 19

Lucia Trimbur enjoys spending time outdoors. ▶

Lucia, a student at Brown University in Rhode Island, was diagnosed with ADD (Attention Deficit Disorder) and mild dyslexia. She is very bright and has a lot of energy, which she uses to help people in need. At Brown, she is part of a special program called Students with Alternate Learning Styles.

When I was a senior in high school, I was positive I wouldn't get into Brown University. But I did. I just didn't have any confidence.

Beginning in the seventh grade, I started to think that something was wrong. I just could not sit still, and I viewed myself as stupid. I thought it was a matter of will and that I just had to buckle down—even though I would study double what other kids did.

In high school, I did really, really bad on my SAT's. So I was tested by a psychologist, although I didn't even know why. When I walked out of the office, I was shocked that they had just told me I had LD. I was diagnosed with mild dyslexia and ADD. The psychologist showed me how my learning pattern was erratic. I scored in the genius range in areas like problem solving, and really low in puzzles. I was upset, and it just confirmed everything I had thought about feeling stupid.

I was then sent to a tutor and a psychologist. The tutor started going over all the stuff I had missed when I was little, like prepositions and punctuation, which affected my writing. I'm also paranoid about going off on tangents in writing, so I learned to make an outline and stick to it. The psychologist showed me how ADD affected the rest of my life. He discussed environments in which I could learn better. Now when I study, I have to go to the library where there are no distractions. He also increased my confidence, so I didn't blame myself for my LD.

In eleventh grade, my friend and I started an environmental and community action club at our school. We wanted to help low-income communities affected by environmental problems and hazards. The club became the most popular one in our school.

This project showed me the benefits of my ADD, and I gained a lot of confidence. Many people with ADD/LD have an energy that's special, and if they can harness it and pour it into something, they can do really amazing things. I have a lot of energy, and I can motivate people. I devoted all my energy to one part of the club project at a time, and that went really well. My coworker was the steady person, which helped when I exploded in different areas.

I received a Feinstein scholarship to attend Brown because of my community work. I'm also on the track team, which has set school records. In

Do you have ADD, like Lucia? If you do, how does it affect your life at school and at home? Can ADD be a positive thing in a person's life? How?

Do you have ideas about ways you can help other people or make a difference in your community? Can you find special projects to focus your energy on?

Lucia, at a high school track meet.

Best School Memory

"Getting all A's in sixth grade and feeling like a good student."

Worst School Memory

"Feeling awful in tenth grade when the English teacher focused on spelling and punctuation errors instead of ideas."

addition, I'm part of a program called Students with Alternate Learning Styles, for students who learn differently.

Another Brown student provides me with help in writing. She's great. She reads all my papers and has taught me how to perfect my outlines. I also get time extensions on all exams and two weeks' notice to complete all papers. I prefer essay tests over multiple choice exams because I do better when I can express my ideas about a concept. Because of my mild dyslexia, I underline as I read and I write notes in the margins. I also try to run before I study because it helps me calm down.

At college, Lucia offers her time and attention to children in need.

The environmental and community action club I helped start in eleventh grade really changed my life. I didn't view myself as a good student—I didn't view myself as anything. But the project was the turning point. I can do something, I really have something that I can give. When I came to Brown, I began to view myself as academic. My classes are so interesting that I don't experience a lack of focus. It's really exciting.

While I'm here, I want to start a shelter to help people who are on the streets get back on their feet and look for jobs. I'm participating in an internship with the World Hunger Program so I can better understand poverty and hunger. After college, I'd like to teach fourth or fifth grade and then run some sort of community organization for kids to go to after school. And if I'm teaching, I'll have the summer off, which is a crucial time for kids. They need a place to go.

"Always have confidence. Find what you're talented at and go for it! Don't shy away from a dream. Stay true to yourself and know that even when things seem hard, you can accomplish anything that you put your mind to!"

Lucia

WHERE'S LUCIA NOW?

I've been in school for most of the last ten years, and currently I'm pursuing a PhD in Sociology and African American studies at Yale. Towards the end of my time at Brown, I didn't utilize any of the LD support services. My biggest problem tended to be concentrating when taking tests. During my first three years, I would be given time and a half, and sometimes unlimited time, in testing situations. The extra time eased my anxiety about testing, so that by the last year of college, I no longer needed extra time. I also think I learned how to manage my workload better at Brown.

I've always felt that what I have is not so much an attention deficit as an attention difference. My sense is that I have a lot of attention for things that I'm good at and enjoy. My academic interests, especially at the graduate level, select for that. PhD work is really great because I can study what I want, and I'm motivated to do the work. Since I'm interested in what I'm studying, I get propelled through my various requirements. I just don't feel bogged down by the idea of LD anymore.

I spent four years doing ethnographic work in a boxing gym in Brooklyn. I study how people who have been released from prison use a boxing gym to reenter society. I look at how they work to get their lives back on track and forge new paths. My dissertation discusses how people reconstitute dignity after various forms of social exclusion and urban marginality. Researching this topic has been a great experience for me—I love the people I work with and the place I did research.

Next year, I have a post-doctoral fellowship at a nonprofit organization in New York City, which will allow me to turn my dissertation into a book. I am extremely lucky in that my friends and I exchange our writing, so I have several informal editors. And, of course, spell-check is essential!

I think it's important for people to follow their passions. Things tend to work themselves out over time—what seems difficult at one point can become a lot easier. If there are particular aspects of school that are interesting, stick with it.

David Collado
Age 17,
and His Band Hogfat

David Collado, rehearsing with his band Hogfat (from left to right: David, Eben, John Paul, Chris, and Zack). ▶

David has a hard time with reading, writing, and organizational skills. He is very talented in video production, computer graphics, and music. David and his friend Zack have formed a band mostly made up of students with LD. David lives in New York, and Hogfat plays throughout the New York area.

David, Vocals

In fourth or fifth grade, I started having trouble writing papers. I was frustrated because I couldn't express what I wanted to say. Organizational skills were also hard for me. Then I was diagnosed as having LD. The testing showed that I had problems with language skills, like vocabulary and understanding what I read.

I went to a language therapist who taught me a lot about language skills. In school, I went to the resource room. Sometimes it helped, but often I wasn't given the kind of help I needed. Math became a real problem, and the school couldn't find the right placement for me. I was in four different math classes during ninth grade. The classroom became a place where I began to feel trapped. It felt like everyone was yelling at me and ignoring the fact that I have LD.

Around the time I was diagnosed, I took a television course in a summer school program. I was interested in movies, and my friend Zack and I used to

Do you get frustrated in class because you feel that people don't understand your LD? How do you act when you're frustrated— quiet, angry, talkative, distant, bored? Can you think of a positive way to handle frustration?

Best School Memory
"Going on TV shoots."

Worst School Memory
"Not being understood by teachers."

David singing with Hogfat.

David, with a video camera at age 12. He has long been interested in video production. ▶

???

Summer is a great time to explore an interest. What summer activities might help you learn new skills?

make movies together starting in the second grade. In middle school, I joined the news show at our school. We'd broadcast live news shows to the classrooms.

I used to work long hours after school with the media specialist, Robert Gluck. When I was in the TV studio, I acted differently than when I was in class. I was more focused, I wanted to participate, and I knew Mr. Gluck cared about me a lot. The TV studio was like a home, and I think the support there kept me going.

Because of these interests, I took a course in media arts at Ithaca College during the summer before ninth grade. I was the youngest kid there, and I created a documentary on today's music. My interest in music grew that summer, and some kids took me to my first punk show. They spiked up my hair, and it was really funny. I liked the fast, aggressive music and the lyrics.

When I came home, my grandmother got me a bass guitar for my birthday. I started taking lessons, and I was in a band with my friend Zack. It was a horrible band. We began to think about starting a band with other kids we knew from the resource room. We created a band called Hogfat in March of '95. I'm the lead singer, and Zack is the drummer.

After ninth grade, I switched to Windward, a school for kids with LD. The change in schools has made me stronger. There are specialized classes for teaching you skills. We have an English class that doesn't just teach you about literature but also teaches you about writing and how to organize yourself when you write. Windward has helped me get adjusted and become more independent.

After school, I work at a place that publishes a college music journal. They review the latest college music, and I help out by doing whatever has to be done. A lot of my free time is spent managing and rehearsing with Hogfat. At first, we were really terrible. Our beat was off, and we didn't have any style.

Then we started listening to other bands that helped influence us. We sound like southern California punk, and we include ska (music of Jamaican origin). We write our own music, and we all play by ear. Four out of the five kids in the band have LD. We wrote a song called "LD," and in our first show we said, "Learning disabled children, stand up and fight. Strike force. It's our right to be learning disabled, and it's all right." We tell the audience that if we forget the words to the songs, it's because we have LD. Our band is great, and soon we're playing our first real Manhattan show.

As the band became more successful, Zack and I started El-Dee Rekords. We thought this would make us look like we had a label and that we were someone. Then people would buy our tapes and listen to our music. I designed the logo, and I've created business cards and newsletters. The artwork for our tape was created on my computer.

In the future, I'll be in a band for fun, but I want to work behind the scenes in the music industry—maybe something video-music oriented. There I could use my talent in music, computers, and video production.

When people hear us, they say, "Wow, these guys have LD and they're musicians, and they can do good stuff." I feel like I've proven myself and people can see that I've accomplished many things. Having LD doesn't mean that we're "stupid," it means that we learn differently than other students. Remember, we are proud to have LD, and you should be, too.

What do you think of Hogfat's words: "Learning disabled children, stand up and fight. Strike force. It's our right to be learning disabled, and it's all right." What do these lines mean to you?

Hogfat's record company is called El-Dee Rekords. Can you guess why?

Zack, Drums

I have ADD (Attention Deficit Disorder), and I have trouble paying attention in some classes, like math and chemistry. I can't sit for long periods of time and focus. Note taking is also hard.

I like being in a band a lot because I like playing and listening to music, especially the type of music we play. The name of the band came from an episode of *The Simpsons,* which is the greatest television show ever made. The LD factor is really cool because it gives us all a sense of identity and a sense of belonging in a group. Our message is that you're not stupid if you're a person with LD.

Eben feels that Hogfat functions well as a unit because most of the members have LD. Do you sometimes feel more "in tune" with your friends or classmates who have LD? Why or why not?

Eben, Bass

I have organizational problems, and I'm horrible in a normal class situation. I sort of tune out, and things go flying over my head. I'm forgetful, and I also have ADD.

I have a lot of fun playing in this band. It's really cool and everything. What's even cooler is I've been in bands in the past, and they didn't function as well as this band. It's probably because we all have LD. We have similarities in the way we see, think, talk, and everything. That's why we function so well as a unit.

Chris, Guitar

I don't have LD, and the learning differences of the other band members don't affect me. There's nothing noticeable about it, and I even think we're more organized than other bands I've been in. This is a great band. Also, none of us think about drugs at all. None of us do drugs—it's not an issue for us.

John Paul (J.P.), Guitar

Being in the band is great. Whenever we have a show coming up, I really look forward to getting up and playing in front of everybody with my guitar. I tend to look past the LD part.

I'm in an alternative program in school where I can learn what I want in class. It's a lot of work, but I'm learning what I want to learn. Some kids use their LD as an excuse, but I think your LD only affects you to a certain extent. After that, it's about trying. Kids with LD have to try harder than most kids.

"If you have LD, you should try to work around it and not think about it. Find an interest and work on mastering it." David

WHERE'S DAVID NOW?

Hogfat broke up when high school ended. My friends from Hogfat are doing well. Eben was in a band called Saves the Day. Chris got married and has two little kids. JP wants to be an electrician. Zack is planning on going to law school and hopes to be a district attorney. I went to NYU Film School on a full scholarship. My mom really encouraged me to go, but I wasn't that interested. The first class was about using a manual camera, and all the math that related to the camera was confusing. I really didn't enjoy going there too much—it was overwhelming, so I left.

I continued doing things I was good at. I managed a band for a while. I took care of the computer systems at Urban Fetch, an Internet company. And I was working with a volunteer fire department, which I had been doing since high school. Then I took tests to become an Emergency Medical Technician. Some of the written tests were hard, especially memorizing the details of the human body. But I passed the tests.

In 1999 I took the firefighters' test to join the New York City Fire Department. My work as a volunteer fireman and EMT helped me to pass the test, especially on the physical part of it. I knew how to throw ladders up, how to pull hoses and drag dummies. Then I got the call to enter the Fire Academy for training. The Academy was a challenge because we had to memorize all the emergency positions for the various types of buildings. I used to look at the buildings on my way home to try and memorize by visualizing them. I passed the tests and started working in the firehouse in January of 2002.

One day my chief asked if I wanted to go into Special Operations. He knew that I was really motivated and offered me this opportunity, even though I had only been in the department for a year. In Special Operations, we deal with all types of hazardous materials emergencies, in addition to the engine, ladder, and rescue work. I've also been to bomb school, live nerve agent school, radiation school, and a rescue school. I've learned how to determine the source of a poisonous gas, isolate and contain it. If someone is trapped under a train, we get it off them. When people fall down holes, we go down and get them. In Special Operations there's a lot of action, and it's exciting.

For me, being a fireman is fun. My LD doesn't stop me. I know that I'm pretty smart and have good street sense. In emergency situations, I'm calm. I'm careful not to get hurt, and if something is too large scale for me, I step back and suggest a plan. All the ups and downs of school have taught me that whatever happens, happens. Things can be fixed. Like the Special Operations' motto states: "Adapt and Overcome."

Dr. Garth Vaz
Age 48

*Dr. Garth Vaz
at his medical
school graduation.*

◀

*Garth has difficulty with reading and writing, but he is
strong in math, science, and understanding people. In
medical school, he was asked to leave because he told a
professor he had dyslexia, and the school thought he
would be incapable of becoming a doctor. Garth refused
to accept that and instead worked hard to show his knowledge. Today, he practices medicine in Texas.*

Do other members of your family have LD? What are their strengths and their weaknesses?

Best School Memory

"The day the academic committee at the medical school decided I had earned my degree."

Worst School Memory

"Being flogged (whipped) for not reading."

I don't know how my mother did it, but ever since I knew I was Garth, I knew I wanted to be a doctor. I think my smart mother brainwashed me! When I was in elementary school and they found out I couldn't read, I thought maybe I couldn't be a doctor. But it was my goal, and I always think about doing the impossible, so I continued to focus.

I did well in my other subjects, was great in math, and was at the top of my class until age 10. When reading became a tool for learning, I started falling behind. In school in Jamaica, where I grew up, I would get a flogging (whipping) for my inability to read. Everyone told me that I was too lazy and that was why I couldn't read. In my family, not being able to read was accepted. That is because none of the males in my family could read. Turns out that they, like me, are all dyslexic.

At home, there were other matters to worry about besides reading. When I was 12, my father stopped supporting us. I would have to find creative ways to get something to eat, such as visit a friend right when it was time for dinner. In Jamaica, you can't really starve because there are so many fruit trees—avocado, pear, breadfruit—and these were my staple meals. There was no money for extra food.

This only lasted a year because then I decided to plant a garden. I also started working to make money. All the things that happen to a person during life are educational. For me, these bad times gave me determination, and I decided that when I grew up I wasn't going to be poor. In the beginning, it was about survival. This pushed me to think about being successful and not to quit when things became difficult because of my LD.

In Jamaica, you go to school to age 15 and then you take an exam to get into a high school. I tried to pass these exams, but I couldn't. Eventually, I went to a school that will accept anyone. In order to pay for this school, you worked on campus. When you had earned enough to cover the cost of the classes, you could begin school. I worked for two years and then began class. After failing my first exam, the teacher said, "Garth, I thought you knew the material." I had participated in class, but I just didn't have enough time to read all the material assigned.

Before the next set of exams began, I quit. Two years of working for just eight weeks of school! While I had been working, I cut my finger in a lawn mower. It was so very painful and bloody that I questioned whether I wanted to be a doctor. I thought I might be too sympathetic to anyone who was in pain and focus on the pain itself, instead of the patient. Because I was good at numbers, I started to think about engineering.

Soon after this, my mother moved to the United States and I went with her. We lived in Brooklyn, New York, and I began to take classes towards my high school degree. I was granted a visa on the condition that I would sign up for the draft. This was during the time of the Vietnam War.

I thought this was fair, because if I had an opportunity to come to the United States, then I should serve in the military. It was decided that I wouldn't go to Vietnam but would serve as a medic in the U.S. Army. I tried to tell the army how I felt about blood, but they said I was going to be a medic. When I began training, my fear of blood went out the window really fast. We saw films about first aid, and I worked in a medical clinic, so I became used to the sight of blood. I began thinking about medicine again and knew I needed an education. So I started studying to pass the GED exam for my high school degree. I was determined to pass this exam because I knew I needed the degree to get into college. After a lot of studying, I passed.

After my years in the army, it was time for college. College was the way for me to get to medical school. I was accepted to a community college in Florida because I agreed to do non-credit courses that would better prepare me, since my high school education was so limited. These classes helped me learn how to manage some of the textbooks. I focused on the pictures, charts, and bold print. I understood what I read, but I was slow. Before each class, I reviewed the material so I would better understand the lecture.

Eventually, I was taking many science classes that would prepare me for medical school. I did really well in these classes and had all A's until I had to take an English literature class. It was the first time I had to write a paper, and I was really floored. Before this, I stayed away from courses requiring writing. I received a C in this class and continued with my plan to get into medical school. I was going to give it all I had, and I studied all the time.

I was accepted to one medical school in Florida with the help of one of my college professors. I had taken so many science classes at the undergraduate level that I was truly prepared for my first two years of medical school. There

Are you studying a lot to prepare for something you want to do in your future?

was lots of reading and, fortunately, there was a note-taking service where other students would take notes for you. That was helpful. During one of my courses, I listened to a lecture on dyslexia. This was the first time I had heard the word, and I thought, "Hmm . . . I think they're talking about me."

I called my brother Donnie about it, and he said, "You know, Garth, I'm dyslexic, too." When a professor asked me about an exam that I had failed, I told him that I was dyslexic. He told me not to tell anybody else because he didn't think the professors at the university could handle it. I couldn't keep it

Garth has a pilot's license and flies all over Texas.

▶

a secret for long because I needed to take a class that required a lot of writing. We were learning how to write about a patient's history, and we recorded the information on a chart. I just couldn't write what I knew was wrong with the patient in a clear manner with proper spelling. This was reported to the dean, and I was kicked out of medical school.

Well, I had always worried about when they would find out that I couldn't read or write very well, and now they knew. This was so depressing, and there were a lot of tears and frustration. However, now that I knew I was dyslexic, I also knew I had legal rights. They couldn't kick me out just because I was dyslexic.

The school asked me to take courses to improve my reading and writing in order to be re-admitted. After I completed these courses, I was allowed back in as long as I didn't fail anything. When I failed a class that I was certain I passed,

⁇

Garth was kicked out of medical school for being dyslexic. Have you ever been treated unfairly because of your LD? What steps did you take to correct the problem?

I was out again. Again I had to prove I was capable, and again I was admitted. This happened a third time, and I knew I needed a plan.

I started taking classes with the professors on the academic status committee, which is the committee that decides whether you can graduate or not. I wanted them to work with me on a one-to-one basis so they could understand that I was smart and that my dyslexia wasn't affecting my ability to be a good doctor. These professors began to support me, so my survival plan was working.

It took me six years to complete medical school, two years longer than average. I was the first dyslexic to graduate from this school. The academic status committee had no clue what dyslexia was all about, and this was a group of doctors. But, you know, the beautiful thing is that they all learned about dyslexia because of me.

I knew from childhood that I was not a quitter. Now I work in a wonderful town called Gonzales, in Texas. The folks in Gonzales think I'm an exceptionally good physician, and I have a successful practice. My patients feel comfortable talking about their problems because they know I am dyslexic and have had my own problems.

Recently, my brother wrote a book about my struggle to become a doctor, called *The Doctor He Begged to Be.* We hope that everyone in this nation will one day have a true understanding of what dyslexia is all about. I think that dyslexics think differently because we have to learn differently. Many successful inventors, discoverers, and entrepreneurs are dyslexic.

As for medicine, I'll be doing it forever. I enjoy being a healer so much. Plus, they pay me for it. After the days of eating from fruit trees, that's a great thing!

Do you work closely with any teachers so that they can better understand your learning style?

Garth holds up the book by his brother Donnie.

"You are probably thinking that things are closing in on you, but consider these problems as the downward thrust of a trampoline that later pushes you even higher. Your problems today will make you a much better person when you grow up."

Garth

WHERE'S GARTH NOW?

My practice has changed over the years. I discontinued obstetrics and gynecology. Now my practice is focused on geriatric medicine, as well as treating kids with learning and behavioral disorders. People come to me because I've talked about my dyslexia. I also had a radio show for two and a half years called "Champions for Children." The show provided information on subjects about kids. The biggest topic was dyslexia, because that's my forte.

I travel a lot and speak about learning and behavioral disorders around the world. To go along with my discussion, I create PowerPoint presentations, but I never present without having it edited by someone else. Once, when I was pressed for time, I asked the audience to edit a presentation with me. They were happy to help me, too.

One thing I do now is use a computer program called Read Please to read to me. It has drastically changed things. I can take in a lot more information this way, so it helps me keep up with the medical research.

I try to speak on a personal level with kids so that they know I understand what they're going through. One patient was reluctant to go to school because he was ashamed that he couldn't read. We chatted, and I shared my experience about how stupid I felt because I couldn't read when I was younger. I helped him to understand that he is not the problem. Our society and the school system are the problems if they are not using the proper method to teach him.

If you want to learn more about Dr. Garth Vaz, check out the book his brother wrote:

The Doctor He Begged to Be by A. McDonald Vaz (McDonald-Vaz Enterprises, 1999). In this book, you'll learn about the struggles Garth faced and about dyslexia. It might help you to think about what you could do to make people across the nation more aware of the challenges of LD.

You can also email Dr. Vaz at gvazmd@aol.com, or check out his website at www.gvazmd.com.

Elizabeth Davis

Age 29

At work, Elizabeth Davis uses a special machine (a TTY) that types messages through the phone to people who are hearing or speech-impaired.

Elizabeth (who goes by Liz) has been diagnosed as dyslexic. She is a strong listener, speaker, and thinker. Despite being told that she would never graduate from high school, she made it all the way through law school. Liz works for the Mayor's Office for People with Disabilities in New York City.

Has anyone predicted (wrongly!) that you wouldn't pass a certain class, pass a grade, or graduate? What was your reaction? How did you prove everyone wrong?

During first grade, I had the feeling that I was not reading the same way as everyone else in class. I kept looking over at the girl next to me to see what I was missing. I just knew I wasn't learning the way I was supposed to be learning. This started to get really frustrating and, after a while, I cried myself to sleep every single night. My mom went to talk to the teachers, but they told her she was a "worried parent."

People were not really aware of dyslexia when I was in first grade. Listening proved to be my strength, and I did very well when I could use my thinking skills. In the later grades, memorizing math facts was terrifying because the flash cards went too quickly. Reading was a challenge. Sometimes I would skip lines or add one part of a word to another part. One of my reading tutors told my mom that I would never go beyond the eighth grade level. Not only did I complete high school, but I also went to college, graduate school, and law school!

By the time I got to seventh grade, I decided I could no longer focus on the actual processes of reading and spelling. Instead, I went to class and listened to the lecture, thought about the information, and contributed to the discussion. So I stopped getting bogged down in reading and figured out a way to get around it. This continued through eighth grade, and I graduated from middle school with academic honors.

I liked the idea of a boarding school, and I received a scholarship to one for high school. This presented a whole new adventure—new people, new environment. During an English class in ninth grade, the teacher surprised me by saying we would take turns reading poetry out loud. I started thinking, "Oh no, I am so scared," because I feared making mistakes when reading out loud. I tried to figure out what stanza I would read, but just then she started skipping around. When it was my turn, I decided to give it my best shot and began, "There was a beautiful bouquet of rhinoceroses." As soon as the word *rhinoceroses* came out of my mouth, I shrank in my seat. I tried to make a joke out of it, but it was horrible. After class, I made a deal with the teacher to tell me in advance when we would read out loud.

High school was hard. Though I was doing fine in most classes in ninth grade, I started slipping in biology. I couldn't read the big words—it was like a new language. One of the teachers took me aside and told me that the school had made a mistake in accepting me, and that I would probably have

During her honeymoon, Liz went scuba diving in Hawaii.

to leave by the end of ninth grade. I cried over that, then worked hard with a friend who helped me pass biology.

However, I did fail Latin and eventually received a foreign language waiver. But I asked to substitute American Sign Language. I thought, "Just because I have a language waiver doesn't mean I shouldn't find another mode of communication." I had actually begun signing when I was 10, as a wonderful way to communicate without the verbal obstacle.

In tenth grade, I was officially diagnosed with dyslexia. I had been advocating for my school needs up until this point, and finally having the word *dyslexia* helped. People understood dyslexia by this time, and using that term now meant that teachers were more willing to listen.

As high school progressed, reading became such a difficult grind for me, and it was hard to get from one page to the next. It actually gave me a headache, and I hated it. But I loved what I got out of it—new information. School became easier as I found more ways to work around my LD. I started using books on tape, and I would listen and read at the same time. I was also careful about not scheduling more than one heavy reading class a semester.

Note taking in class was hard, and I asked friends to go over the parts that I had missed. My friends also helped by proofreading all my papers. When I needed a teacher to make an accommodation (special option) for me, I was

What do you think about Liz's reaction to her foreign language waiver?

Best School Memory

"Walking away from high school, college, and law school with a diploma in hand."

Worst School Memory

"Reading the word *rhinoceroses* instead of *rhododendrons*."

Do you belong to a study group? Or, do your friends help you with homework and preparing for tests? What kind of support network do you rely on?

very straightforward. I never asked to get out of something; I would never, ever do that. Instead, I offered an alternative and explained why that alternative was a better option. If I received extra time on an exam, I was proportionately just as rushed as the person who didn't have extra time, because it takes me twice as long to read. This was not an advantage but an accommodation, so that I was not at a disadvantage. It allowed me to be tested on what I knew, rather than on how quickly I could skim the question itself.

When I applied to college, I made sure I chose a place that had an Office for Disability Services. When you go to a new school, you have to start all over again with understanding the new school requirements and how it affects your LD. I went to Barnard College, which had a structured support service. The LD specialists offered to send letters to my professors explaining that I may need accommodations. I never used those letters. I preferred to go to the professor the first day, introduce myself, and explain my needs.

I described to my professors what I needed in order to be successful. Some of them needed some pushing, but I stood my ground by offering alternatives. I was going to walk out of there with something that was going to work for both of us. It was my right to do it. Study groups, note-taking services, composing on the computer, and books on tape were all necessary means for me to succeed.

When the reading material was so voluminous that there was no way for me to get through it, I learned to read the first and last sentence of every paragraph. This could not give me a complete understanding, but I learned enough to be prepared for class so that I could actively participate and follow the discussion, thus learning by listening.

I wanted to go to law school because I felt it gave me the best opportunity to reach the goals I had set for myself. I planned to study disability law because of my own experiences. Law school was an entirely different animal, and there was no way to tame it! The school was much more rigid, and there aren't many dyslexics who go to law school, probably because the reading load is so great.

Law school was not as flexible for me, and some people felt that if I had made it to law school, then I must have "gotten over" my dyslexia. Again, I relied heavily on the note-taking service, which allowed me to use my strength of listening in class. Study groups were my absolute savior because there was no way I could do all the reading. My study group friends understood my LD so well that they would know which sections I would have difficulty reading. I still had to learn the material—they just helped me learn it. There were times when it was so intense I thought I would have to leave, but I did graduate and I am indeed a lawyer.

Liz celebrates her graduation from law school, with her husband, Luis.

Ultimately, I took a job working in the New York City Mayor's Office for People with Disabilities. I'm Assistant to Counsel, so I do work on legal issues. However, I still have one major hurdle left—passing the bar exam. It is a grueling exam that lasts four days because I need extended time. I have taken it and have not yet passed it, but I will!

I am also a Senior Policy Analyst. I make sure that the rights of people with disabilities are protected. I got a master's degree in deaf culture while in law school, this enables me to better understand the needs of others. My experiences fighting for what I needed throughout my own education have helped me to appreciate the needs of others with different disabilities.

Though my disability may be hidden, it still affects me every day. At work, I use a special computer that can "read" documents to me. I also ask someone to proofread my memos before I send them out. Because of my experiences, I am often asked to speak to students with LD. I tell them to acknowledge their differences but EXPLODE when demonstrating their abilities.

What do you think Liz means when she says, "EXPLODE when demonstrating your abilities"?

"Work hard to reach your goals and stand up for what you deserve. Most importantly, thank your parents, your brothers and sisters, your teachers, and your friends for all their support and encouragement. Be well, be confident, and dare to be true to yourself."

WHERE'S ELIZABETH NOW?

In 1997, while I was working in the Mayor's Office for People with Disabilities in New York City, I got a call that changed my career. There was a situation in which sixty-four deaf Mexicans were found enslaved. I was called in to help because of my knowledge of disabilities and sign language. I was able to quickly assess the problem and suggest the kind of emergency support needed. Soon after, I was transferred to the Office of Emergency Management (OEM) as a Special Needs Advisor to the Commissioner and Mayor. I was hired because of my ability to identify the needs of people with disabilities in an emergency situation and find creative but realistic solutions.

After this, OEM began to recognize special needs issues when planning for emergencies. This job was a natural fit for me because of my knowledge of disabilities. My LD did not impact my ability to function in this field. If anything, it gave me better qualifications to speak on behalf of people with disabilities. Additionally, my legal training helped me to analyze situations and quickly understand them. I stopped thinking about passing the bar because it was irrelevant to what I was doing.

I was with the OEM through September 11th. When the World Trade Center was attacked, we quickly responded to the situation. After surviving the collapse of the tower, we made sure that the emergency response plans for senior citizens and people with disabilities were set in motion. I learned many lessons that day, especially that preparedness correlates to survivability for everyone—with and without disabilities.

Eventually I left city government to spend more time with my family, while offering my services as a private consultant. The demand for my expertise was so great that I now run my own company. My firm specializes in emergency management and special needs—not one or the other, but both. When hurricane Katrina struck, people with disabilities were terribly affected. Our analysis of that situation led to new emergency management procedures for the future.

In July 2004, a presidential Executive Order was signed, recognizing the inclusion of the needs of people with disabilities in emergency planning. I was invited to the White House for the signing, which was an honor. Finally, at the presidential level, special needs in emergency management is a central issue.

Running my own business fits perfectly with the strengths in my style of learning. Of course my LD still exists, it never goes away. But since the business is mine, I can work around my issues. Having my own firm brings out my talents. Each of us should look to accentuate our strengths and in no way allow anyone to make determinations about our future. People see that I am passionate about what I do because it is so much a part of me.

If you want to learn more about Elizabeth's company, please visit www.eadassociates.com.

Learn More About LD

Ten Questions and Answers About LD

Many people have questions about LD. That's perfectly natural because it can be hard to understand that a smart person can have trouble learning.

If you want to find out more about learning differences, there are many ways to get information. For example, if you're a teacher who works with students who have LD, you can take special classes, read books on the subject (see pages 123-124 for suggested books), attend conferences, and ask questions. If you're a parent whose child has LD, you can also do these things, or you can contact special organizations for more information (see pages 125-126 for a list of organizations).

If you're a student with LD, learn all you can about LD and don't be afraid to ask questions. You can find answers to your questions in books, from videos, and on the Internet (see pages 120-122 and 127 for resources). Following are answers to ten of the most commonly asked questions about LD:

1. What is LD?

The Learning Disabilities Association of America says LD " . . . affects the manner in which individuals with normal or above-average intelligence select, retain, and express information. Incoming or outgoing information may become scrambled as it travels between the senses and the brain." In other words, when you have LD, the information that goes in or comes out of your brain can get mixed up, making learning or expressing information more difficult. For more information about the Learning Disabilities Association of America, see page 125.

2. How many people have LD?

Experts report that between 4 and 10 percent of the U.S. population have LD, though some reports estimate even higher numbers. That means millions of children and adults have LD.

3. Who has LD?

Anyone can have LD, whether male or female, young or old. People of all races and backgrounds can have LD. LD often runs in families, so more than one family member may have learning difficulties.

Studies have shown that more boys than girls have LD, but experts believe that there are probably as many girls with LD as boys. However, girls' learning difficulties are often different from boys' and are sometimes harder to diagnose. One reason they are more difficult to diagnose is that girls are usually better behaved at school, so their learning problems may not be noticed as easily.

4. What is the most common form of LD?

Dyslexia, which affects about 75 to 85 percent of all individuals who have LD.

5. What is dyslexia?

Dyslexia is a language-based learning problem. It mainly affects learning to read, spell, and write. People with dyslexia may also have problems with spoken language and math.

6. What are other kinds of LD?

There are many other kinds of LD. For example, some people with LD have a hard time memorizing information. Other people with LD may have trouble with organizational skills. Here are some other kinds of LD:

- *Dysgraphia* is a problem with written language.
- *Dyscalculia* is a problem with mathematics.
- A language-based learning difficulty is one in which there is mainly a problem understanding or using the spoken language.
- A nonverbal learning problem can cause difficulty in understanding social situations.
- Fine-motor weaknesses are seen when a person has trouble using a pencil or perhaps tying shoelaces.
- Gross-motor weaknesses cause a difficulty in playing sports.

7. What is Attention Deficit Hyperactivity Disorder?

Attention Deficit Hyperactivity Disorder (ADHD) is a difficulty in keeping attention focused, sitting still, and/or thinking before speaking or acting. A person with ADHD may or may not also have a learning difficulty. Children who have ADHD may also have it as adults, though ADHD can disappear during the teenage years.

8. How do you find out if you have LD?

Usually a parent or teacher notices that a student is having trouble in one or more subjects. Together, the parents and teacher decide to have the student tested by experts who understand LD. The tests can show if a student has a learning difficulty, and can help parents and teachers better understand the student's learning needs. The tests can also suggest teaching methods that might work best for the student.

9. What teaching methods work best with students who have LD?

Students with LD tell us that their minds work differently, and it helps when they are taught differently. Most students with LD learn best when new information is presented so they can see, hear, and even touch it. Students with LD often find it helpful when a teacher presents a small amount of information at a time. Before moving on to the next topic, teachers should check that the students have understood the information.

10. Does LD ever go away?

LD may exist over a lifetime. But with expert help, people who have LD can learn ways to build on their strengths and make up for their weaknesses. As seen in the stories in this book, some people with LD believe that their learning difficulties have helped them to succeed.

Ten Ways to Succeed with LD

The people who shared their stories for this book worked hard to reach their goals. But hard work isn't the only thing that got them where they are today. Many of them used survival skills, like the ones described in this section. If you have LD, read through the list and think about whether these ideas could help you. You can photocopy the list and put it in your notebook to look at whenever you need to. If you don't have LD but you know someone who does, show the list to that person. He or she might really appreciate your support.

1. Find and use resources.

There are many resources available to people with LD: special schools, LD programs, resource rooms, special education classes, LD experts, tutors, and more. Find out which resources are available to you, then use them! Remember that using these resources doesn't mean you're "stupid"—it means you're smart enough to get the help you need.

2. Find strategies that work for you.

Do you need time extensions on projects and tests? Do you need to use a computer or a calculator to complete your work? Should you have a helper proofread your work to spot errors? Whatever you need, don't feel ashamed about asking for it. You're not trying to get out of doing the work, you're just trying to do the best job possible.

3. Be honest about your LD.

Having LD doesn't have to be some big secret. There are people who can and will help you learn and give you the support you need—teachers, parents, relatives, coaches, tutors, mentors, counselors, friends, and so on. Let them know about your LD.

4. Don't use your LD as an excuse.

Just because you have LD doesn't mean you're doomed to fail or do poorly. You may, however, have to work harder to succeed. Saying, "I can't do my homework because I have LD," or "I can't possibly pass this class because of my LD, so what's the point in trying?" isn't fair to you or to your teachers. Remember, you may learn differently, but you can still learn.

5. Be aware of your rights.

Don't be afraid to speak up if you don't think you're getting the help you need or the education you deserve. You can talk to a parent, teacher, school counselor, school social worker, your principal, or any other adult you trust.

6. Find an interest, hobby, or activity you enjoy.

Instead of worrying or getting angry about your LD, spend time doing something you love to do. Whether it's sports, building things, dance, art, or starting a business, the activity can take your mind off your troubles and will help you learn new skills.

7. Focus on your strengths.

Feeling sad or upset about what you *aren't* good at isn't the answer. Instead, work on what you *are* good at. Then practice, practice, practice. Exploring your talents to the fullest will help you and others discover what's really special about you.

8. Keep trying.

Everyone hits obstacles sooner or later, so don't feel like you're the only one. You may fail a test after studying for days, you may find you're not getting the academic help you need, or you may run into someone who treats you badly because of your LD. No matter what happens, don't give up!

9. Learn more about LD.

Find out as much as you can about LD and your learning style. This will help you at home, in school, on the job, and in life. If you become an expert on your own LD, you can help other people to understand you better, and you'll help yourself.

10. Believe in yourself.

Positive self-esteem is one of the greatest motivators of all. If you feel confident, if you believe you can succeed, there's no stopping you!

Resources for Students

Books

I Wish I Could Fly Like a Bird! by Katherine Denison; Wildwood Creative Enterprises (1996). This is the story of Chic L. Dee, a bird with learning disabilities who flip-flops when he tries to fly. While he struggles to accept his limitations, he begins to discover his talents, trust his intuition, and find his own way. Perhaps most importantly, he learns about making room for differences. This is fun reading for children who also struggle with learning disabilities.

Eddie Enough! by Debbie Zimmett; Woodbine House (2001). Meet Eddie Minetti, human whirl-wind and third-grader. He thinks, moves, and speaks quickly and it often gets him into trouble. For anyone who is the parent, friend, or teacher of a child with Attention Deficit Hyperactivity Disorder (ADHD), *Eddie Enough!* rings true. Share this book and its happy ending with grade school children with ADHD, their siblings, and playmates.

The Survival Guide for Kids With LD: Learning Differences by Gary L. Fisher and Rhoda Cummings; Free Spirit Publishing (2002). First published in 1990, this survival guide has helped countless young people labeled "learning disabled"—and the adults who care about them. Meanwhile, laws have changed and technology has advanced. This revised and updated edition retains the best of the original edition: the warmth, affirmation, and solid information kids need in order to understand that they're smart and can learn, they just learn differently.

The Alphabet War: A Story About Dyslexia by Diane Burton Robb; Albert Whitman and Company (2004). Adam starts school, and although he loves stories, he can't seem to get the words to make sense. Over the next few years, he slowly despairs of ever learning to read. Instead, he imagines that he is being held captive by an evil king who torments him with vowels. His parents hire tutors to help, but it isn't until a specialist comes in at the beginning of third grade and diagnoses him as dyslexic that things start to look up.

The Don't-Give-Up Kid and Learning Differences by Jeanne Gehret; Verbal Images Press (1996). A children's book with much needed encouragement for kids with LD or ADHD. Describes a young boy with dyslexia and how he learns to cope with it.

Joey Pigza Swallowed the Key by Jack Gantos; Harper Trophy (2000). Joey is a kid who bounces off the wall, sometimes literally. He just can't seem to get a grip on his behavior. Joey knows he's really a good kid, but no matter how hard he tries to do the right thing, something always seems to go wrong. Will he ever get anything right? A National Book Award Finalist, this book paints a realistic and hopeful picture of life with ADD.

We Can Do It! By Laura Dwight; Star Bright Books (2005). We can do lots of things. So proclaim the five preschoolers that we meet in this book. Gina has spina bifida, David has Down syndrome, Sarah is blind, and Jewel and Emiliano have cerebral palsy. But that doesn't stop any of them from playing, learning or laughing. Glossary and resource list included. Also available in Spanish. *We Can Do It!* is a wonderful resource for children and their parents and teachers who are learning about the special needs of their classmates.

Thank You, Mr. Falker by Patricia Polacco; Philomel (1998). Little Trisha is overjoyed at the thought of starting school and learning how to read. But when she looks at a book, all the letters and numbers just get jumbled up. Her classmates make matters worse by calling her "dummy." Only Mr. Falker, a stylish, fun-loving new teacher, recognizes Trisha's incredible artistic ability and her problem, and takes the time to lead her finally and happily to the magic of reading. This autobiographical story is close to author Patricia Polacco's heart. It is her personal song of thanks to teachers like Mr. Falker, who quietly but surely change the lives of the children they teach.

The Hank Zipzer Books by Henry Winkler, Lin Oliver, and Jesse Joshua Watson; Grosset and Dunlap (2003-2008). This fourteen book series was inspired by the true life experiences of Henry Winkler, who is remembered as "The Fonz," among other roles. The main character, Hank Zipzer, is the world's greatest underachiever. His experiences are funny and touching, and the authors deal with learning differences in a gentle and humorous manner. Boys who struggle in school will especially appreciate these stories, but the enjoyable, fast-pased novels will draw in other children as well.

Recordings, Videotapes, and DVDs

Recording for the Blind and Dyslexic
20 Roszel Road
Princeton, NJ 08540
Telephone: (866) 732-3585
email: custserv@rfbd.org
www.rfbd.org

An extensive lending library of books on audiocassette for people who are blind or who have reading difficulties. The collection includes educational books in all subjects, for ages 9 up.

Hello Friend
Ennis William Cosby Foundation
PO Box 4061
Santa Monica, CA 90411
(800) 343-5540
email: info@hellofriend.org
www.hellofriend.org

"Ennis' Gift: A Film About Learning Differences" is a video and DVD used by educators and parents to promote understanding and positive approaches towards children who learn differently. This film has been broadcast on both HBO and public television around the country.

The Lab School
4759 Reservoir Road NW
Washington, DC 20007
(202) 965-6600
www.labschool.org

Ask for "LD Stories 1, LD Stories 2, and On the Edge." Videos by Lab School students use animation to show what it's like to have LD.

Resources for Parents and Teachers

Books

Overcoming Dyslexia by Dr. Sally Shaywitz; Knopf (2003). From one of the world's leading experts on reading and dyslexia, a comprehensive, up-to-date, and practical book to help understand, identify, and overcome the reading problems that plague American children today. Drawing on recent scientific breakthroughs—many of them in her own laboratory—Dr. Shaywitz demystifies the subject of reading difficulties and explains how a child can be helped to become a good reader.

Attention, Memory and Executive Function by G. Reid Lyon and Norman A. Krasnegor; Paul H. Brookes Publishing (1996). Incorporating different theoretical perspectives, this book helps establish some common understanding of these three central processes, while research findings also can aid clinicians in assessing and remediating reading and attention disorders.

A Parent's Guide to Special Education by Linda Wilmshurst and Alan W. Brue; AMACON (2005). Offers guidance to parents and their children—as well as to teachers, counselors, and administrators—on issues including diagnosis and awareness; special education laws; eligibility issues and requirements; programs; parenting issues; and communication between parents and schools.

Learning about Learning Disabilities, Third Edition by Bernice Y.L. Wong; Elsevier Publishing. (2004). A summary of current research on learning disabilities, which covers ADHD, memory, language processing, social competence, self-regulation, and brain structures as they apply to learning disabilities. Chapters also focus on instructional aspects of learning disabilities, including teaching literacy, reading comprehension, writing, and mathematics.

It's Nobody's Fault by Dr. Harold S. Koplewicz; Three Rivers Press (1997). People who wouldn't dream of blaming parents for a child's asthma or diabetes are often quick to blame bad parenting for a child's hyperactivity, depression, or school phobia. The parents, in turn, often blame their children, believing that they're lazy or rebellious. Even worse, the children with these psychological problems often blame themselves, convinced that they're just bad kids. In *It's Nobody's Fault*, esteemed child and adolescent psychiatrist Dr. Harold S. Koplewicz at last puts an end to this pointless -- and erroneous -- cycle of blame and helps parents get the support they need for their troubled children.

Socially ADDept: A Manual for Parents of Children with ADHD and/or Learning Disabilities by Janet Z. Giler; C E S Continuing Education Seminars (2000). Through a series of exercises and suggested dialogue, *Socially ADDept* helps parents teach the hidden rules of communication to children who are having social problems, such as how to handle teasing, use appropriate body language, comprehend jokes and sarcasm, and join groups effectively.

Learning Outside the Lines by Jonathan Mooney and David Cole; Fireside (2000). Written by two "academic failures"—that is, two academic failures who graduated from Brown University at the top of their class, Jonathan Mooney and David Cole teach students how to take control of their education and find true success—and they offer all the reasons why students should persevere.

Dr. Larry Silver's Advice to Parents on ADHD by Dr. Larry Silver; Three Rivers Press (1999). With this fully realized second edition of the classic guide, Dr. Larry Silver addresses the subjects all parents wonder about when they suspect their child has attention deficit hyperactivity disorder such as what causes ADHD, how to obtain an accurate diagnosis, and what's the latest information on medications and other treatments. Dr. Silver's warm, thoroughly practical guide will give parents, teachers, and others the support they want and the answers they need.

To Be Gifted and Learning Disabled: Strategies for Helping Bright Students with LD, ADHD, and More by Susan Baum and Steven Owen; Creative Learning Press (2004). Thoroughly researched and filled with case studies, practical suggestions and techniques for working with GLD students, useful resources, and much more, *To Be Gifted and Learning Disabled* is a resource for anyone who works or lives with a child who has both startling talents and disabling weaknesses.

Games for Reading: Playful Ways to Help Your Child Read by Peggy Kaye; Pantheon (1984). Peggy Kaye's *Games for Reading* helps children read by doing just what kids like best: playing games. These games are fun for the whole family and will help most beginning readers—including those who have reading problems and those who do not—learn to read and want to read.

Finally, though they are mostly out of print, any book by Priscilla Vail will help inform parents and teachers alike about kids with LD in a practical and heartfelt manner. Priscilla Vail (1931-2003) wrote with a lively, easy to read tone that made difficult to understand disorders understandable. Check out any of the used book websites to find new or used copies of her books.

Organizations*

American Speech–Language–Hearing Association (ASHA)
2200 Research Blvd
Rockville, MD 20850
Telephone: (800) 638-8255
email: actioncenter@asha.org
www.asha.org

A professional and parent organization that focuses on communication disorders. Publications, workshops, and conferences are available.

CHADD (Children and Adults with Attention Deficit/Hyperactivity Disorder)
8181 Professional Place, Suite 150
Landover, MD 20785
Telephone: (800) 233-4050/(301) 306-7070
www.chadd.org

A national nonprofit organization for parents and professionals, CHADD offers support and promotes awareness of ADD.

Council for Exceptional Children (CEC) Division of Learning Disabilities (DLD)
1110 North Glebe Road, Suite 300
Arlington, VA 22201-5704
Telephone: (888) CEC-SPED/(888) 232-7733
(703) 620-3660
www.cec.sped.org

An organization dedicated to advancing the quality of education for all exceptional children and improving the conditions under which special educators work. The Division of Learning Disabilities focuses on LD.

Council for Learning Disabilities (CLD)
11184 Antioch Road, Box 405
Overland Park, KS 66210
(913) 491-1011
email: CLDInfo@ie-events.com
www.cldinternational.org

A national organization that serves professionals working with individuals who have LD.

The International Dyslexia Association
40 York Road, 4th Floor
Baltimore, MD 21204
(410) 296-0232
www.interdys.org

Formerly known as the Orton Dyslexia Society, this professional and parent member organization offers programs, publications, and supports research Irelated to dyslexia. Chapters are located in most states, and there are international branches as well.

Learning Disabilities Association of America (LDA)
4156 Library Road
Pittsburgh, PA 15234-1349
(412) 341-1515
www.ldanatl.org

A nonprofit volunteer organization for individuals with LD. Membership includes people with LD, their family members, and professionals devoted to advancing the education and well-being of children and adults with learning differences. Publications are available through the national and local chapters.

*NOTE: Because websites change often and without notice, we can't promise that every address on this list will still be accurate when you read it. When in doubt, use a search engine.

National Center for Learning Disabilities (NCLD)
381 Park Avenue South, Suite 1401
New York, NY 10016
Telephone: (888) 575-7373/(212) 545-7510
www.ncld.org

An organization for parents and professionals that promotes public awareness and understanding of children with LD. NCLD also has an extensive referral system, educational programs, and numerous publications.

U.S. Department of Education
Office of Special Education and Rehabilitative Services
400 Maryland Avenue SW
Washington, DC 20202
(800) USA-Learn/(800) 872-5327
www.ed.gov/about/offices/list/osers

Provides information on special education laws and related services. Contact your State Department of Education (in your state capital) for further information at the local level.

Websites*

LD OnLine
www.ldonline.org

LD OnLine is the result of a collaboration between public broadcasting and the learning disabilities community. This site offers reliable information about LD and ADD, a national calendar of related events, artwork and writing by young people with LD, audio clips from experts, recommended resources, and more.

LD Resources
www.ldresources.org

This site contains a variety of resources for the LD community. Includes links to essays and articles about LD, information on LD and writing, and LD resources.

Resources for Giften Children with Special Needs
www.uniquelygifted.org

The Uniquely Gifted site is a collection of resources for families with gifted/special needs children and the professionals who work with them. It includes information on resources, web sites, advocacy groups, assistive technology, and more.

SchwabLearning.org
www.schwablearning.org

Schwab Learning was founded in 1989 by the Charles & Helen Schwab Foundation as a community service for parents, families, and others seeking resources on learning differences. Their site offers a parent journal, media articles, educational programs, information on LD organizations, support groups, physicians, speech and language specialists, and more.

Special Education Resources on the Internet (SERI)
www.seriweb.com

The SERI project is a collection of Internet resources for those involved or interested in special education. The site includes information about learning disabilities, national organizations, resources for parents and educators, special education discussion groups, links to many related sites, and much more.

*NOTE: Because websites change often and without notice, we can't promise that every address on this list will still be accurate when you read it. When in doubt, use a search engine.

About the Author

Jill Lauren has a B.S. and M.A. in Learning Disabilities from Northwestern University. She currently conducts a private practice for teaching LD students in New York City and consults with parents and schools.

Jill has been teaching LD students of all ages since the early 1980s. She has also trained regular education and special education teachers in effective teaching methods for students with LD. She believes that educators who listen carefully to older students with LD will receive valuable information about the teaching methods that work best for them. Jill especially loves teaching young children to "crack the code" and read.

The idea for *Succeeding with LD* came from one of Jill's students. Jill likes hearing about success stories, and she met the young people profiled in the book through teacher recommendations. In her free time, Jill enjoys outdoor sports, exploring nature, and traveling around the world.

For more information about Jill Lauren, please visit her website at www.jilllauren.com.